THE Re-Mating Game
Dating & Relating In Middle Life

Max L. Marshall

BETTERWAY PUBLICATIONS, INC.
WHITE HALL, VIRGINIA

D1474854

Published by Betterway Publications, Inc.
Box 219
Crozet, VA 22932

Cover design by Deborah B. Chappell
Copyright C 1988 by Max L. Marshall

Library of Congress Cataloging-in-Publication Data

Marshall, Max L.
    The re-mating game.

    1. Dating (Social customs) 2. Mate selection
—United States. 3. Divorced people—United States.
4. Widowers—United States 5. Widows—United
States. I. Title II. Title: Remating game.
HQ801.M372 1988   646.7'7   88-19375
ISBN 1-55870-109-5 (pbk.)

Printed in the United States of America
9 8 7 6 5 4 3 2 1

To my daughter, Connie

ACKNOWLEDGMENTS

I would like to express my appreciation first of all to Joel Mixon, who did such a splendid job of editing my manuscript. Also, my thanks go to John Ianno, Katie Maxwell, Joyce Rothschild, and Gwen Esch for their valuable comments and suggestions; also to Carl and Judy Meissner, who provided input concerning divorce adjustment counseling. James Doran's contributions, support, and his personal friendship were most helpful, as were the contributions of Ted Hacker, Frank Lawton, Florence Niwinski, and the docents at the Salvador Dali Museum. Jane Olson's Adventure Travel Club and the Clearwater chapter of Parents Without Partners (especially under the Presidency of John McGatha), as well as the St. Petersburg chapter, served as valuable home bases for me while I was adjusting to single life; I owe them a debt of gratitude for many happy hours.

I especially want to thank Velma Wright for her encouragement, enthusiasm, helpfulness, and editorial assistance.

October, 1988, M.L.M.

Contents

Introduction

As with millions of other men and women, time, along with the tides, eventually eroded what had been a long and, I thought, happy marriage — the last few years excepted. The reality of divorce, and the isolation and loneliness that came with that painful territory, hit me hard. I wanted to stop the world so I could get off, and it took some time for me to recover.

When I did recover, I decided to make lemonade out of the trainload of lemons that divorce had dumped in my backyard. I would use my past training and new experiences to write a book on the subject of dating, relating, and remating that would help me get my life together again and would be useful to others as well. I thought this was an original idea until I got into my research. Apparently hundreds — for all I know, thousands — of articles and books have been sparked by the same motivation.

The cover of the January 8, 1988 issue of *The Tampa Tribune* weekly entertainment magazine *Friday extra!* featured a Barbie Doll being asked for a dance by a male counterpart at a singles bar. The headline read "The Singles Machine," and the subhead, "Entertaining ways to help you meet a mate." (Singles bars are about the worst place to look for a mate, and Chapter 9 tells you why.) An article inside by Marilyn A. Gillen titled "The Meet Market" suggested that a supermarket might be a good place to find someone on a Friday night and offered pointers on how best to wheel a cart up and down the aisles while looking for love. Here's some advice from this apparently tongue-in-cheek article, suggesting you do your opposite-sex shopping around the fresh vegetable bins:

> "Look at it this way," Laurie, 24, says with the force of a general instructing a raw recruit. "Everywhere else in the store, you just whiz by and pick up what you need — a can of soup here, a bar of soap there. Right?" she asks, and pauses to see that the point is well taken. It is.
> "But here," she continues, and her eyes flash with the fervor of someone about to reveal a universal truth while

her hand waves a cucumber like a sword. "Here you have to stop, park your cart, and spend some time. It's about the best place in the whole store to actually get to talk to someone. Especially by the weird stuff that nobody knows what it is — you get to ask around."

Well, there are a lot better places to go to meet people, as you will discover from reading this book. You'll also learn that there are a number of hurdles that newly divorced or widowed people must successfully negotiate so they can readjust and go on to lead reasonably happy lives. The first is getting over the emotional debilitation that comes with the stark realization that you are suddenly alone in the world — a frightening jolt. About the time of my divorce, some eight years ago, most of the books on the subject of divorce dealt with this topic, and they did help me to regain my emotional balance.

However, there was a paucity of good books with guidance for the day-to-day social life of singles. Dating may make you a nervous wreck, but if you want to relate or remate to someone new, you quickly realize that dating is where it all must begin. Where *were* all the women (men)? How do you meet them? What is the best way to get a date? What do people do on dates nowadays? What do they talk about? How have changing mores affected sexual practices? What about relationships, especially "meaningful relationships"? What about remarriage? How about singles vacations? What's Club Med like ? Should I take a singles cruise? What about singles bars, dating services, and even classified ads?

This book, divided into four parts, is intended to provide newly single mature adults with a map of the new terrain they are about to traverse as well as some practical advice on how to negotiate it — how to successfully date, relate, and (maybe) remate.

Part I, REAL WORLD, contains information about emotional adjustment, dating practices, and the various risks involved (especially regarding sex). Also included is advice on self-improvement, so that the reader may become healthier, more interesting, and more dateable and relateable. Singles clubs and singles travel are described in Part II, SINGLE WORLD. Part III, CASUAL WORLD, deals with the quicker and easier (and riskier) approaches to singles dating: the singles bars, dating services, "mating services," and classified personal ads. Part IV, AS YOUR WORLD TURNS, addresses "Love and Remarriage" from the mature single's point of view.

1.

Saturday Night is the Loneliest Night

After the end of a twenty- or thirty-year marriage, the thought of dating again can make anyone nervous and even resentful of the need to start all over again. For weeks I was frozen into inaction, not knowing what to do and fearful of rejection. Just the word "dating" brought on an acute anxiety attack. I didn't know that this reaction was common.

OVERCOMING FEAR OF DATING

Middle-aged men and women who have the greatest initial difficulty in dating are probably those who are suddenly and unexpectedly divorced. Their self-esteem and self-confidence are often eroded, and their fear of rejection temporarily limits their ability to take risks by either asking for or accepting dates.

I perceived myself as something of a wallflower, with little ability to relate to the opposite sex. I also mistakenly believed that all the people I saw at parties or dances were having a good time, that they knew exactly how to act and exactly what to say. I believed myself to be the only miserable, lonely, and socially inept person in the world.

Fear triumphed for a seemingly endless period, and I couldn't muster the courage to date for several weeks. When I did date, I botched it. I was searching for another wife. I wasn't even comfortable with dating, and there I was wife hunting. As a consequence, I was scaring women away. It took some time before I was able to stop thinking of every woman I dated as a possible replacement spouse.

Another trap that may hold you back — it did me — is thinking you are, and always will be, a poor date. You may very well be a poor date at first; many people are. This too is completely natural, but the more experience you acquire in dating, the sharper your dating skills become.

In the beginning, try to date without becoming emotionally involved with any particular person. After several months, when the numbness of single-shock subsides, you may be ready to profit from an intimate and exclusive relationship. But that's down the road, not right away.

STARTING OVER

If your experience parallels mine, you will hurt for a while no matter what you do. It simply takes more time to mend a broken heart than a broken arm. For a few weeks or months, it may be all you can do just to survive. But as soon as you're able, get out and develop some new interests. You may have noticed that old friends are already beginning to disappear from your life. Replace them with new friends who reflect your new situation.

When asked, "Where do I start?" I advise people to read some of the divorce or death adjustment literature available. Some of the good books have been around a long time, like *Games Divorced People Play* by M. Berke and J. Grant. It contains some technical jargon but has many sound insights into why we do what we do. Mel Krantzler's books, *Creative Divorce* and *Learning to Love Again*, have both been helpful to successive waves of the newly divorced.

A few books on the market will be of little use and are perhaps even counterproductive. You can spot these when the thrust of the advice is oversimplified, when easy solutions are offered for complex problems, or when quick results are promised. Realize that adjusting to your loss and building a new life will take time and that easy choices usually result in difficulties. All too often the inexperienced give credence to cliché slogans to justify their past behavior and express unrealistic hopes for the future. Some who assert they are "finding themselves" are just groping in the dark, barely coping, and sinking in emotional quicksand. And we hear so much about being "free and independent." We all- need people, and most of us are happiest in a close relationship with someone else. Beware of facile books and glib acquaintances who recite such misleading nonsense.

Another step is to sign up for seminars for the newly divorced or widowed. These classes are offered in most communities either by colleges, churches, or family service organizations. By expressing your feelings during these seminars, you will experience a surprising lift in your spirits. Also, you will hear the experiences of other singles in similar situations, and listening to their challenges and frustrations, you will realize that you are not alone. When moderated by experienced instructors, these workshops offer a great deal of valuable information, not to mention possible new friendships.

We seldom seek substantial change in our lives when life moves along satisfactorily. The trauma you may be suffering provides an excellent opportunity to start making a new life and a new you. Begin turning negatives into positives by identifying a few new interests and activities you want to pursue and regularly attending the classes or meetings. Not only will you enlarge and broaden your interests, you will create the opportunities to meet other single people, both men and women, in comfortable, non-threatening environments.

THE IMPORTANCE OF DATING

In six months to a year, some of these new acquaintances will become enjoyable common-interest friends in your new lifestyle. Also, some will be dates, some will be "relates," and in time, perhaps there will be that special someone you will mate or marry.

All the while, force yourself to be open to dating. Dating will usually be just as nerve-wracking as it always was, and if you're a mature parent with kids in high school, college, or beyond, you may very well have a tendency to ask yourself, Who needs this?

You do! You need to start dating if you want to restore some semblance of the social life you once knew and enjoyed. If you eventually want to relate to someone again in a meaningful way, it has to start with dating. Whatever your long-term or short-term goals, they inevitably begin with dating.

WHERE NOT TO LOOK

Keep in mind that dating is one thing and getting into a serious relationship or remarrying right away is quite another. More than anything right now, you need time to heal, to catch your emotional breath, and to regain your social balance.

The newly single will be wise to heed some other caveats; among them, avoid picking up dates in bars. Becoming physically entangled with strangers will almost inevitably subject you to further pain and discouragement. The right things will begin to happen if instead, you force yourself to get involved in activities, classes, sports, and special-interest groups where you get to know the people you meet. Naturally, your chances of meeting people to date will be best if you join those groups which include many singles, so don't forget the singles clubs and the singles travel clubs. They facilitate all aspects of socializing, meeting people, and dating again.

CASUAL WORLD, SINGLE WORLD, REAL WORLD

In time you will come to realize that single people move within a universe of three constellations, each with its own obstacles and rewards. There is the Casual World of one-night stands, of which the bar scene is most representative; there is Single World, typified by the various singles clubs; and there is Real World, encompassing the myriad of special-interest activities and organizations in which all people engage, not just singles.

My advice is to start by becoming simultaneously active in the latter two, Single World and Real World. Then resolve to go out with decent people from both of these worlds whenever an opportunity arises, if for no other reason than to learn the what, where, and when about dating nowadays — to practice and get used to dating again.

One of the quickest and easiest ways to meet people and find dates — though not necessarily the best of mates — is to join one or two of the singles clubs which flourish all over the country. They provide meeting grounds for the growing divorced population, and for widows and widowers as well. Join and attend the functions of one or two of these clubs, but also pursue a few Real World activities, such as a bicycling club or church group. Do both regularly as soon as you can drag yourself out of the house.

In the singles clubs, just as in other social circles, you will run across people who share a few of your interests. As elsewhere, simply make friends with the people you like, remain pleasantly neutral to those you feel indifferent toward, and maintain a courteous distance from strangers you find offensive.

While singles clubs and singles travel clubs can help you stake out a new social life more efficiently, don't spend all your leisure time in them; pursue other avenues simultaneously. More often than not, a better meeting ground for high quality new friends is found in interest and activity groups. The Real World consists of sports and exercise groups, cultural activities, educational courses, hobby clubs, religious affiliations, museums, political organizations, work-related functions, and much more — just about anything that interests both single and married people from all walks of life.

PRACTICE MAKES PERFECT

In the beginning, while you are trying to learn the ropes and relearn dating techniques, don't be overly choosy. As long as a person is known by you or your friends or relatives to be presentable and of good reputation, date him or her. Remember, you're only looking to date at first, not to remate. So be ready and willing to take advantage of every dating opportunity. Again, consider these dates as practice — practice for the "important" dates ahead.

Whatever you do, try not to view your early dates as potential spouses. Concentrate on trying to polish your old dating skills. If you're like the majority of us, you'll be nervous. This uneasiness is typical of longtime married people thrust into single life, so accept early jitters and realize that the more you date, the less nervous you'll be. Your aim is to get out of the house and out of yourself. Be aware that there isn't all that much new under the sun about human nature or about dating. The way you dated before is usually the way middle-agers date now.

Because their experiences and tastes are often more varied and well defined than when they were younger, middle-agers sometimes tend to be more adventurous. Yet looking for dates still requires courage. I can tell you where to find dates, but you must gather your resolve and get started. Force yourself to do so. Ignore the sweaty palms, the pounding heart, the fear of rejection, and the occasional panic. They all come with the territory.

DATING ACTIVITIES

What do people do on dates? The same as always: They meet for coffee, or drinks, or a meal. They go to a show, go dancing, maybe go to a ball game, or to the beach. Whatever they do, they get to know each other through conversation. Any setting is a good one, therefore, if it enables a couple to talk freely. If you are meeting someone for the first time or barely know him or her, drinks or coffee is a very appropriate way to get acquainted.

A movie date provides an excellent setting for shy couples. For two hours you're in the company of another person without the stress of having to fill the time with conversation. After the movie, it's natural to stop for a cup of coffee or a drink, and the logical opening topic of conversation is the movie.

Dating someone from the Real World with whom you share a common interest is your most comfortable option. Quite often you'll have mutual friends and acquaintances to talk about or to go out with. Not only is it fun to do things with a group, it is also easier to talk casually to the opposite sex in group settings. Moreover, by joining special-interest organizations you get an opportunity to go out with the group even when you don't have a date. So resolve to join a few groups engaged in the things you like to do. Do you like to sail, bowl, or ride a bike? Or do you prefer less strenuous activities such as playing bridge or going to art galleries?

Last but not least, keep your eyes (and mind) open on the job and in your neighborhood for possible dating opportunities. Ask a co-worker to have coffee with you during a break or to go for a walk with you in a nearby park. Having lunch with someone also is casual and non-threatening. After all, everyone has to eat. Keep the conversation light and positive. Even when you feel down, try not to talk about your troubles, especially the "war stories" of your marriage. Smile a lot and try to see the humor in things.

WHOM TO DATE

You can more easily relax with someone you are not strongly attracted to romantically or consider to be a "prospect." Dating an old friend you feel old-shoe comfortable with can conceivably lead to pleasant surprises down the road and also serves as excellent "practice." Keep in mind, however, that new friends are out there waiting to be met.

Early on, attempt to identify the kind of person you prefer to date. Like so many things, attitudes have changed. For example, many women are more independent. They don't need men to be the focal points of their lives. If you're a man, what's your reaction to that type of woman? If you're not comfortable with her thinking, you might save yourself some discomfort by avoiding the "liberated woman." Plenty of traditional women are out there, if that is your preference. On the other hand, you may indeed prefer the less traditional women. There are also traditional and not-so-traditional men. To each his (or her) own. Whomever you choose to date, be pleasant and respect his or her philosophies.

Think of your early dates as being exactly what they are — exercises in spending time with someone you don't know very well. By talking and doing things together, you are experimenting with new relationships. Avoid thinking about your possible future together. Remind yourself that you are going out mainly for the experience of dating.

BEING YOURSELF

If you are unsure of what you should or should not do and say on a date, do and say what comes naturally. Concentrate on having a good time without anticipating what might go wrong — or right. With time and experience you'll know what to do, and the only way to get experience is to keep dating. When you date someone compatible whom you enjoy being with, first just try to become friends. Moreover, don't necessarily judge a person by your first date. He or she may have been nervous or had a bad day at work. If you like the person, give them another chance.

Be yourself. If you say something or do something stupid or awkward, your date will probably overlook it. It's not the end of the world, and most people intuitively understand. As you gain dating experience, the awkward moments and seemingly stupid mistakes will occur less often. Experience leads to confidence, and confidence leads to social ease and skill.

DATING IN "DESIRABLE" CIRCLES

You may have to force yourself to go out and find dating opportunities, and a particularly determined effort is often needed to meet the kind of people you consider especially desirable. Remember that those who move in the same social circles often kindle romances which bloom into caring and committed relationships. Therefore, consciously and purposely join the social groups in which you expect to find the type of people you really want to date. Meanwhile, however, keep dating others for the practice as soon as you can force yourself to go out. If you decide to wait until you meet only the most "desirable people," chances are you will wait forever. As you gain experience dating, you may be surprised by how your ideas about "desirability" change.

When you attend singles club functions — discussions, parties, dances, and outings — keep fixed in your mind the fact that everyone is there for precisely the same reason you are: to meet and date members of the opposite sex. Moreover, many are hoping to relate to another person on an exclusive basis, and of these, most hope eventually to remate. The people you see and meet in singles groups are generally ready, willing, and available to date. Couples tend to drop out. Understandably, you will not be the answer to every person's dream, just as you certainly won't find many of the people you meet in singles clubs to be representative of your ideal.

ENJOYING DATING

In time you will become much more relaxed and comfortable in any social situation, and you will become a more interesting person and therefore a better date. Dating skills, like almost all skills, are learned; they improve with knowledge and practice. At first you may feel awkward, but as you date more you will gradually notice a change.

All this doesn't happen overnight, or after a few dates, or even after a few dozen dates. In time you will discover what mature people in your circles do on dates, what they talk about, where they go, and how they handle themselves in various situations. You will slowly begin to feel comfortable. Without really being aware of it, you will begin to relax more when you go out, and you will have a reasonably good experience each time — and so will the people with you.

What will have happened is that you have "grown" — a word much overused with the result that its meaning has been obscured. Essentially, personal "growth" merely means positive change. It means self-improvement, increased self-awareness, overcoming or minimizing hang-ups, and, in general, becoming a more well-adjusted person. The potential is always there — we all have room to improve ourselves.

OF COURSE IT HURTS

When you suffer the negative emotions of anger, fear, and depression, keep reminding yourself that these feelings are natural when you are alone, particularly if you have been abandoned and badly hurt. However, tell yourself repeatedly that it is unhealthy to dwell on your emotional miseries and get mired in the quicksand of feeling sorry for yourself. Action, not introspection, is what is called for to get back on track toward a reasonably happy life.

Newly single people need to ventilate their unhappiness but sometimes they unload on anyone who happens to be on hand. Try to spare your dates. Except for heart-to-hearts with good friends and family, resolve to stop telling your troubles at every opportunity. Force yourself to remember that regardless of how ill-treated you might have been prior to a divorce, anger, resentment, self-pity, and guilt — however justified — are expensive luxuries few can afford. Besides, they definitely turn people off. Once in a while you may lapse on a date, but remind yourself that you're on the date to get out of yourself, to have fun, and to relearn dating skills so you'll be ready for Mr. or Ms. Reasonably Right when he or she comes along.

Mature men and women tend to be understanding, and if for some reason they can't (or don't want to) accept an invitation for a date, they usually refuse without thoughtlessly destroying the other person's ego. Asking a friend to go out is nerve-wracking enough; asking is even more difficult when the prospect is only an acquaintance and the possibility of rejection is high. While many women still wait to be asked, men have the difficult problem of asking, of putting their egos on the line. (In typical relations between the sexes, the man initiates the relationship, the woman controls the way it develops, and either one can terminate it.) Newly divorced men are particularly vulnerable. Their self-esteem has often been bruised and their self-confidence may be at a low ebb. Getting started again socially is not easy for them.

MAKING YOURSELF ATTRACTIVE

Facing the challenge of making a new life for yourself is up to you; no one is going to do it for you. Think of life as an adventure. It is, of course. Begin by making yourself as physically healthy and attractive as possible. This involves developing and maintaining a healthy, well-toned body and a well-groomed appearance. It's a fact of life, right or wrong, that appearances count. If you need improvement in the physical area, check with your doctor and begin now. Many health clubs, by the way, are great places for singles of all ages to meet.

Aside from making yourself physically attractive and grooming well, try to project a happy and confident outlook. Cultivate a pleasant attitude; good feelings inside reflect on the outside. While this is difficult to accomplish when you're feeling miserable and depressed, the next two chapters will suggest some ways to help you eliminate or minimize your negatives and accentuate your positives. Don't expect overnight results, however. Like learning how to date again, this may take a little time.

FOR MEN MAINLY

How do you approach a woman to open a conversation? It depends on the occasion, but icebreaker techniques follow more or less established patterns. At a singles club rap session, for example, let's say the woman who interests you contributed to the group discussion. After the rap, comment on something she said. Did you agree or disagree with her? Elaborate on it; the conversation will flow from there. If you can't think of a thing to say and no such entry exists, simply force yourself to approach her. Introduce yourself and tell her you're new to the club. You can always ask her how long she's been a member. If asked, be agreeable to joining a group for coffee or a pizza after the rap session. If you've met a woman you're attracted to, ask her along.

Almost a must for single people is knowing how to dance. If you don't know how, learn. Since today's dance steps are unregimented and almost any dance floor maneuver is acceptable, it's easy to get by. Do you have a woman friend who is a good dancer? Ask her to give you some pointers, or take lessons. Singles clubs often offer lessons, or try the YWCA or YMCA. Dance studios are usually very expensive, but they do an excellent job of teaching ballroom dancing and offer a unique opportunity to meet women.

Of course, you can always go to the singles club dances and not dance. If you're comfortable with just mingling, move around to the various tables. Feel free to ask a woman to go out for a drink or coffee afterwards, even if you don't ask her to dance. Such spur-of-the-moment dates help you to get to know people with little cost in nervous tension.

For relative strangers, dinner at a restaurant facilitates conversation but can be expensive. Save your resources for that special someone. "Putting on the dog" for each of your first-time dates can leave you still owing the landlord halfway through the month. If you do dine out, choose the restaurant, in part, for atmosphere. A greasy spoon is obviously out, and a fast-food place is not going to do much for your image. On the other hand, don't forget about the cost. If the restaurant is too expensive, you're going to be nervous about the bill, and she might be nervous about what you'll expect from her later. When this happens, neither of you can relax. What might have been a pleasant evening turns out to be one you're glad is over.

If you are in poor economic circumstances (not uncommon among the newly divorced), don't let your temporary situation keep you from dating. Simply choose inexpensive things to do. A visit to a museum or art gallery might be very appealing to a woman you've been wanting to date. A free film at a local library might not delight everyone, but there are those around who would be pleased with the idea. How about a walk along a nature trail or a trip to the zoo? Almost everyone enjoys these kinds of activities. Even a leisurely stroll through a shopping mall, window shopping and checking out the attractions, can be an inexpensive way to spend some time. Topping off the date with a cup of coffee or a drink at a local bar can result in one of those low-key but very enjoyable evenings — at minimum expense.

On the other hand, if you're financially sound, don't skimp when you go out. If you enjoy the theater, by all means go. After the play, go ahead with the gourmet restaurant if you want to and can afford it. Whatever you decide to spend on an evening's entertainment, feel good about that amount. If you feel comfortable, so will your date. Spend more than you can afford and your date will sense your nervousness.

Follow the golden rule in your behavior toward dates. Make a conscious effort not to hurt any woman you go out with. Remember, the woman you date may have her hands full with her own emotional crisis. She could be as vulnerable as you are, and loneliness can be overwhelming. Don't say things you don't mean. If you tell a woman you'll call her, then call. Most importantly, don't promise relationships that you don't plan to enter. If you lie to a woman, you not only hurt her but you hurt yourself — word gets around. Make your date feel good about herself. Make a special effort if she is newly single; her self-esteem probably needs a boost. Since women talk to each other, you'll come to be known as a straight shooter, someone who plays fair and is up-front and honest in his association with others.

FOR WOMEN MAINLY

You won't be single long before you realize that single women outnumber single men. Even though there is one newly divorced man for every newly divorced woman, those statistics change rather quickly. Many middle-aged men prefer being with younger women. That's one of the main reasons singles clubs have a preponderance of women. Another reason is that men more than women tend to shy away from these clubs. Nevertheless, there are many ways to improve your odds. The most obvious is simply to spend as much of your time as you can where there are lots of eligible men.

The advice about learning to dance is as valid for females as it is for males. I hope you've read the section FOR MEN MAINLY, because it contains much that is also applicable to women and will help you to understand the dating problems men encounter.

While seeking to adjust to single life, you can get help from experienced acquaintances at the singles clubs. You will find that women are far more supportive of one another than their male counterparts are. If you are newly single, make the effort and you'll soon be rewarded. A good friend who knows Single World can be worth her weight in gold. She's been where you're going and knows some of the pitfalls — and some of the joys.

Be active in those circles where you can find and attract eligible men. Don't apologize to yourself or to anyone else for giving preference to activities in which there are more eligible men in good socio-economic circumstances. For example, you might take a junior college course in investments, a class well attended by men. At mid-session break, instead of seeking refuge with the few women who might also be attending, try to stay with a mixed group. Subtly convey the impression that you are friendly and approachable. Then say yes if you are asked out for coffee afterwards.

Sometimes early dating opportunities come out of the blue from longtime friends or acquaintances. Keep an open mind and be inclined to say yes. For example, one evening while she is peeling potatoes for dinner, a woman's telephone rings. Instead of hearing the familiar voice of a family member or friend, or the saccharine salutations of somebody trying to peddle something, she hears the friendly but slightly nervous voice of a male acquaintance at work. Soon she realizes that he is going to ask her out, and she too feels a little nervous. She's never thought of him as a potential date; they've hardly spoken. She's smiled at him whenever they've passed in the hall — as she does to everyone else — but she doesn't know much about him, only that he has a good reputation and that most people seem to like and respect him. On the other hand, she's never considered him as someone special, and he's not particularly good looking. He would hardly stand out in a crowd and is just an average kind of guy. What should she do?

If she's wise, she'll force herself to overcome her unconscious, fear-induced impulse to say no and give an excuse. She'll accept. It's a date, maybe her first date since the roof caved in. The important thing at this stage is not so much who the person is or even where you are going. The important thing is to start going out. Perhaps the fact that she is in no way enamored of him will make the date easier for her.

While you are looking for a man you can relate to, don't sit home alone. Either at work or in your interest groups or singles clubs, you'll meet other women who have similar backgrounds and interests. Go out and do things with them. The one thing you want to keep in mind, though, is not to be so surrounded by women that men are deterred from speaking to you. Just be your friendly self — to both men and women.

An important word for all women to remember is "no." "Yes" is certainly in order at times, but "no" is there for your protection. Use it when you have doubts about becoming involved. While it is a fact that men nowadays don't expect mature women to be prudes, they don't usually take women seriously who are promiscuous. Many men can't help bragging about their conquests. Consider this along with the risks associated with venereal disease and AIDS in making your decision. Refusing sex on a first date is a good idea, even if you are really attracted to the man and feel ready and willing. Think ahead and decide what you want to do and when. A woman who goes out on a third date with a man should not be surprised, however, to find the matter of sex on the evening's agenda. Know what your response will be. Advance planning makes it easier to say no or to say yes.

MEN TELEPHONING WOMEN

The fear of rejection is an impediment that begins with the very thought of telephoning to ask for a date. Ann Landers once suggested that a reticent man calmly resolve to call any five unattached, single women — not movie-star types — just ordinary, decent women who move in the man's interest groups, workplace, or singles club circles. You're practically assured of a date; Ann wouldn't lead you astray. If you can't think of any eligible women, let alone five of them, then read the chapters on how to meet singles and how to use the singles clubs.

What about the mechanics of telephoning for a Saturday night date? The experience can be nerve-wracking for the novice. Learn from the experiences of seasoned singles: Before calling, decide exactly where you want to go and how much you want to spend. This way you can give enough details over the phone so that she will know how to dress. If dinner is what you have in mind, give her a choice between two specific restaurants. If she isn't free on the evening you've chosen, suggest an alternative date. If the answer is either a polite or evasive no, end the conversation. You might say something to the effect that you enjoyed talking to her and perhaps another time. Then call the next woman on your list.

If you are turned down by more than one woman, don't feel that your manhood and self-worth are on the line. Nothing is on the line. If you are realistic you know to expect turndowns. Any woman you call might be busy, might be involved in another relationship (or trying to develop one), or might be too beset with personal or family problems to have time for a social life. It is also true that she might simply not consider you her cup of tea. So what? Hang up the phone and call someone else.

What if you are refused over and over again? Either you are exhibiting one of the negative traits discussed in the next chapter, or you are overreaching yourself. If you are the Ernest Borgnine type, yet repeatedly invite out the Loni Andersons of this world, or if you are elderly yet always telephone the young, perhaps you are asking to be turned down.

WOMEN TELEPHONING MEN

Contrary to what you will often hear at singles raps, for a woman to pick up the telephone and call a man she doesn't know is usually ill-advised. Nevertheless, some women do successfully arrange first dates on the telephone by using tact or guile. One ploy commonly used is: "My boss gave me two tickets to the play tomorrow night. Would you care to join me?" (Your chances would be better if the tickets were for the Super Bowl!) As with men, there is always the risk of being turned down. Remember, rejection hurts even after a considerate, tactful refusal.

I've observed that if men are asked publicly, especially in mixed company, whether or not they are favorably inclined toward women phoning for a first date, most of them will offer little objection. Some might sidestep the issue by saying it would depend on the woman, or they might imply that it's okay, or even say it's fine. But when I asked several men privately how they really felt about women taking the lead, most of them were uncomfortable with the idea. In the real world, contrary to the fantasy world of TV commercials, it is not "downright upright" for a woman to telephone and invite a man over for a glass of Bristol Cream — that is, unless she knows him and they have an established relationship. If this is the case, then go ahead and call; there's no reason not to.

Many women don't realize that men usually pick up the phone with sweaty palms when calling for a first date. Usually a man will be more inclined to call if he has received some encouragement. If you like a man, be especially friendly to him and make it as easy as possible for him to ask for your phone number. You might even say that it would be nice to hear from him.

TO BED, OR NOT TO BED...

Regardless of how nice or expensive an evening's entertainment, a woman should not feel obligated to go to bed on a first date, or on any subsequent date. By the same token, a man should not feel he is insulting a woman if he doesn't make advances. Sexual decisions are very private and individual. Explore your own feelings on the subject and act accordingly.

Sexual mores — and risks — have changed drastically from those that prevailed during our early dating years. It used to be that there were "good girls" and "bad girls," girls who "did" and girls who "didn't." Today, most women "do," at least sometimes. Casual sex is widely practiced, especially in places like Hollywood and particularly by professional singles who either don't want to get married or haven't been able to find mates. Although promiscuity is still frowned on by most mature adults, enjoying sexual relations within a steady and exclusive relationship is frequently acceptable.

Many single couples enjoy sex together until they either marry or sever their relationships. But there are risks — health risks and emotional risks. Intimate sexual closeness often goes hand in hand with commitment, and if you are ready neither to give nor to accept commitment, then perhaps you would do better to refrain. We are all familiar with the increased health risks; there will be more about this in the next chapter.

SHARING DATING EXPENSES

More than just sexual mores has changed, so has the economics of dating. Today women are more inclined to share dating expenses when they can afford to. In particular, many couples who date regularly are comfortable sharing the costs of the more expensive events. In fact, when one or the other doesn't carry his or her fair share in one way or another, the relationship will often encounter difficulty and probably founder. People don't like to be used and will not put up with it indefinitely.

Still widely accepted is the practice that the person who initiates the date pays all the expenses incurred on the date, and the man usually suggests what to do and where to go. Even so, women should bear in mind that they don't have to go places they dislike or to neighborhoods where they may be afraid. One of the purposes of deciding where to go beforehand is so the woman will know how to dress, but another is so she can refuse the date altogether, depending on what the man has in mind. Moreover, if he has invited her to do one thing and then later switches signals by proposing something else, she should refuse if she doesn't like the alternative.

SOME WORDS TO THE WISE

Summarizing my suggestions to the suddenly single who would like to start dating again, I recommend that you:

1. Read some articles and books about divorce or death adjustment and look around for seminars.

2. Make yourself as physically attractive as possible through good grooming, dress, diet, and exercise.

3. Join one or two singles clubs to get out of the house and facilitate early dating and socializing.

4. Befriend experienced singles you like and can relate to. Listen to their advice and benefit from their experience in Single World.

5. Position yourself in social, educational, cultural, and sports or exercise groups in which you can meet desirable dates.

6. Put on a sunny smile and be friendly in your dealings with everyone.

PULLING PEOPLE TOGETHER

There is no escaping the fact that most sensible dating, relating, and remating goes on between people who have something to offer each other. Three important attributes which attract and hold middle-aged, middle-income people to each other are: (1) physical attractiveness and sexual desirability, (2) socio-economic-cultural status, and (3) personality and character. If you take a fairly accurate inventory of where you stand in each of these key dimensions, you will know what you have to offer.

Frequently, however, the newly single of both sexes begin their dating efforts by either greatly underestimating themselves or by carrying around grossly inflated opinions of themselves. The inflated ones often think they should be dating the reigning beauty queen or some rich and handsome Adonis. Sooner or later they learn that water seeks its own level. On the other hand, those who underestimate themselves may form liaisons with just about anyone. Feeling desperate, they are likely to go out with people demonstrating unacceptable behavior or having serious psychological problems. They will blindly ignore the wisdom in the old advice, "Never get involved with someone who has more problems than you do."

When you get right down to it, these suggestions offered to help mature adults play the dating game contain nothing new or startling and may well resemble advice you recently gave your teenage children. Closely examined, they more or less encompass the old dating skills you practiced years ago. The principles you practiced when you first dated are still applicable today; they are merely set to slightly different and faster music. Knowledge about what to do on dates is not the main problem. It is, rather, summoning the courage to do it, making the effort to meet new people, and then letting experience help you become comfortable in your new social environment.

2.

Be Careful, It's My Heart (and Health)

Once you begin to emerge from your social cocoon and start dating, you may be tempted to enter into a relationship. Be careful, and don't rush into intimacy prematurely. Beware of the natural tendency to become involved with the first person who comforts you. It's easy to do. All those outrageous slings and arrows you and your former spouse probably flung at each other still hurt. It feels good to be near someone who apparently cares, and primal instincts begin to stir. But wait, several months if possible — even a year.

You'll soon discover that the sex life of a single person is different from what you were accustomed to when you were married. The opportunity to have sex whenever the two of you were in the mood no longer exists. Instead, physical gratification is a hit-or-miss affair. There will be periods when nothing much occurs, and there may be times when more is available than you can handle. Beware of entering into a relationship solely for sex; this handicaps you in getting to know other eligible partners. But if you do get into a relationship that is wrong, shake loose from it. Don't consider it another failure; it's not. Many singles find their way in and out of several liaisons before settling down with Mr. or Ms. Reasonably Right. Keep the number of liaisons to a minimum, however; the risks of venereal disease are escalating these days.

The way a newly single person handles his or her sex life can be a real pitfall. The fact that a marriage has ended obviously doesn't put an end to physical and emotional needs, but there are healthy and unhealthy ways to proceed. What is appropriate depends largely on individual values, morals, and religious convictions. Go slow in any case, and err on the side of caution.

First and foremost, be true to yourself. Be true to your feelings and maintain your personal moral and ethical standards. If you try to model your behavior on that of other singles whose values you don't really share, you'll be miserable. Positive, healthy change occurs gradually, not overnight.

MAINTAINING MORAL AND ETHICAL VALUES

Suppose a woman named Margaret was raised with the belief that sex was permissible only within a marriage. Let's say she remained true to that belief for her entire married life, yet now she has strong sexual needs and urges. Her friends tell her to loosen up. "Be free," they say. "This isn't the Dark Ages."

Margaret's first allegiance is surely to herself, but part of her is constrained by the strong beliefs she grew up with and part of her wants to change. She wavers in her feelings. When listening to her friends, she agrees with what they say. Why not seek a sexual partner? But when she's alone and thinks it over, she knows that jumping into bed right away is not for her. Perhaps the day will come when she will feel differently and will want to follow her friends' advice, but for now Margaret decides to forego a sexual liaison. Instead, she opts to spend six months or so meeting as many single men as she can and pursuing some old and some new interests.

Margaret is a wise lady. She knows that change is part of life, but that positive change within ourselves comes gradually. She doesn't act hastily on the tempting new ideas she hears, but realizes that new ideas are meant to be studied, bounced around, and only then accepted or discarded. Next year she may think differently, but for now she is comfortable with her decision, wisely basing her actions on her current values. She may feel a lot of pressure from her friends and dates, but her well-considered personal conviction will give her the courage to say no until she is really ready to say yes.

ABRUPT LIFESTYLE CHANGES

Margaret has her opposites. The literature on divorce abounds with instances in which people abruptly begin to behave quite differently. They suddenly do an about-face, completely changing their lifestyles and sexual habits — for all the wrong reasons. Some men encounter an irresistible need to prove their sexual prowess to themselves and to the world. Some women, by the same token, need to prove to society (and sometimes to their former spouses, of all people!) that they are physically attractive and sexually desirable. Usually such promiscuity exacts a heavy toll, both physically and emotionally. Only rarely do people who jump into bed at every opportunity attain anything approaching peace of mind.

Again, when it comes to sex, proceed slowly. There's no particular virtue in remaining chaste for a lifetime after being divorced or widowed, but neither is a silver cup awarded for high marks in promiscuity.

There are, however, plenty of booby prizes for those who seek awards in the sexual numbers game. Aside from the increasingly serious risks of disease, the accompanying stress to prove his manhood can make a man impotent, while a woman also can become sexually dysfunctional. Moreover, the stress on both men and women will exact a toll emotionally and psychologically.

Take the time you need to learn about single life and the various lifestyles it encompasses. Definitely don't get seriously involved the first year. If you follow this course and are patient and prudent, then friendships, dates, good sex, healthy relationships and, possibly, a happy remating will all follow in due course.

V.D. AND DESTROYED LIVES

If you follow a swinging lifestyle, particularly one involving alcohol or drugs, much more than ever before you are tempting fate because of the widespread dangers of AIDS, herpes, chlamydia, syphilis, and gonorrhea. Engaging in sex with multiple partners is dangerous to your health — and plain stupid!

Contract AIDS and you're dead — along with some of the people with whom you have been intimate. A woman can become sterile from pelvic inflammatory disease; PID is serious business. Catch herpes and you've got it for life. How you relate to the opposite sex and how you experience sex is impaired thereafter. If you're interested in eventual marriage, your prospects are vastly diminished, if not eliminated.

Regardless of your long-range goals, dating in the here and now becomes complicated. What do you do when the time, the place, and the person are right but you're worried you might catch something? Cross your fingers and go ahead? How safe is "safe sex"? What do you say when a relationship is evolving and a potential sex partner asks you if you are healthy? Do you become indignant? If it was ever true that sexual intimacy involved relatively little health risk and that frequently changing sex partners was only part of a game like musical chairs, it absolutely isn't true in today's world.

Unless you decide to abstain completely, you will need to take some reasonable and calculated risks in seeking to fulfill your needs, and it's only prudent to keep the odds high in your favor. Now more than ever before, you need to get your bearings in single life and get to know people as friends before you hop into bed. Love is not necessarily a prerequisite for sex, but you should certainly like and respect the person, and this is usually not possible after only one or two dates. Haste may waste you.

DATING AND RELATING

Soon after you begin dating you may discover that you are comfortable with someone and having a good time. The world no longer looks bleak. This usually happens the first time you think a special person has entered your life or maybe the first time you've had sex again. If nothing comes of the relationship you'll feel let down, but keep in mind that you've already met one good person and will doubtless meet others. Chalk it up to experience, but learn from the experience. When Mr. or Ms. Reasonably Right does come along, you'll be better prepared.

After a number of dates with different people and perhaps after a few relationships, you will become a more knowledgeable single, better able to make friendly acquaintances of the opposite sex. If your goal is eventually to find a new mate, chances are that one of these encounters will in fact result in marriage — but hardly ever as soon as some overly eager singles would like. Quite often a more or less satisfactory interim solution is found: a long-lasting, exclusive relationship offering emotional support, intimacy, and help with such mundane chores as hanging the drapes. There is constant companionship, a shoulder to lean on, and a body to cuddle up to.

As in marriage, these relationships may be characterized by a lifestyle that is not very exciting, but they are usually a lot more comfortable, safe, and satisfying than going it alone. Comfortably ensconced in such a relationship, you won't be alone on Saturday nights and you'll have someone to share the holidays with. In addition to safe sex, you'll enjoy many warm and happy evenings when you merely visit, talk, and maybe watch television together. The excitement and stimulation of a lively single life may be just great, but in large doses it soon becomes boring and unsatisfying. Some relationships you may enter will be of short duration, especially the early ones; others may last for years, even a lifetime. Sooner or later some are transformed into marriages. Other couples who might lose alimony, pension rights, health benefits, or other entitlements, opt to live together — without the piece of paper. Some people have found clergymen who will marry them in "God's Eye." Although religiously sanctioned, such unions are not legally binding.

Some men and women perpetually move from one relationship to another, dating casually in between. This is sometimes by choice, as in the case of many career-minded people, but frequently by necessity, as with many singles addicted to alcohol or drugs, socially handicapped by obesity (not just ten or twenty pounds overweight), or suffering from psychological or emotional problems. Typically they date many people for brief periods, with a rare relationship thrown in from time to time. With adequate support from family and friends, their chances of leading reasonably satisfactory lives improve with the progress they make in overcoming their shortcomings.

DURATION OF RELATIONSHIPS

While you can easily obtain information concerning where to find dates and what to do on them, there are no precise blueprints for developing and conducting a good relationship. It is a creative act entered into by two people, and it involves a mixture of chemistry, intuition, personality, and enlightened self-interest. In a good relationship the partners become close friends, if not best friends. Each strives not only to fulfill his or her own needs, but also to fulfill the needs of the partner.

All relationships have a beginning, a middle, and an end — even lifelong happy ones. Accept the fact that there are relationships of short, medium, and long duration. After you've gone with someone for a while, your relationship may end for any number of reasons, even though the two of you are generally compatible and share many values and interests. A broken relationship is painful, but the risk is well worth it. Remember, we all learn from our mistakes.

One reliable catalyst for the disintegration of a relationship is sexual infidelity. Although this comes as no surprise with regard to marital estrangement, most people don't realize that it takes a large toll in single life as well. Unfortunately, some singles who had unfaithful spouses will avoid exclusive relationships altogether rather than risk the pain of a repeat performance. Unlike many of their younger counterparts, most middle-aged singles reject the notion that their different needs can be met by different people. They don't want one partner for sex, one for companionship, and one for intellectual stimulation. Experience has convinced them that these separate parts do not add up to an emotional whole. (Actually, with the increasing threat of AIDS and herpes, younger people are also tending more toward exclusive pairing.) Anyone familiar with the world of singles has seen people loudly proclaim the joys of the carefree, fun-filled single life only to turn around and get married at the first opportunity.

Relationships vary greatly. They vary by their duration, and they vary by the depth of feeling the partners have for each other. They vary in the amount of passion, and in living arrangements.

There are relationships of convenience just as there are marriages of convenience. Relationships can be loving and caring, or they can be superficial and exploitive. There are those in which only one partner is in love, and there are "open" relationships, just like "open" marriages and usually just as unstable and short-lived. In relationships that are destined to evolve into permanent pairings, the partners not only become involved in each other's hopes, dreams, and ambitions, but they also help each other cope with mundane problems and depend upon each other for all kinds of mutual support.

UNREALISTIC EXPECTATIONS

One thing a relationship between the sexes never encompasses is perpetual bliss accompanied by glamorous excitement. For that illusion you need to stay home and watch television, go to the movies, or read a book. On the covers of the singles magazines I subscribe to I inevitably see laughing, happy couples engaged in some ecstatic activity. They are either dressed in formal clothes and dining at a fine restaurant, or they are laughing and playing practically naked on some beautiful beach while the surf rolls merrily in the background. Sometimes they are dancing in the moonlight, and if they are dining, it is always by candlelight. Of course they always have beautiful faces and perfect bodies.

These magazines really ought to caution their readers that any resemblance between the people on their covers and flesh-and-blood single folks is purely coincidental. Glamor, like magic, seldom enters our lives. Only in our fantasies can it exist perpetually. Anyone contemplating divorce because of dreams of finding Shangri-la in the world of singles would do well to sit down, calm down, and maybe back down.

WHEN A RELATIONSHIP ENDS

You will be lucky indeed if your first close relationship leads to a happy remarriage. More often than not, it will end after a few months or maybe even a few years. How you react will play a role in how quickly you recover and how much you continue to "grow," that is, improve in a positive way.

Nothing can be gained by blaming the breakup exclusively on your former partner. Chances are you contributed too, perhaps significantly. Don't let anger and resentment remain in your thoughts for long, poisoning your emotions and hampering good relations with others. Don't become preoccupied by the wrongs inflicted on you by the "ingrate" you once loved, if only for a while. Let your ex-partner worry about cleaning up his or her side of the street. Get out a broom and start working on yours.

Begin by eliminating the negatives, and then go on to accentuating some of your positives. The following two chapters contain helpful suggestions for improving yourself — and your dating and relating abilities. Please read them after you've finished this chapter. Don't skip ahead to some of the more "interesting" chapters.

CONTEMPLATING DIVORCE? A WORD OF ADVICE

A cautionary word is in order for those readers who are not yet divorced but who are contemplating ending their marriages. Be aware, as I have said, that any image you may harbor of romance and adventure with eager and attractive new partners in a glamorous and exciting singles setting is usually a delusion. Be leery of divorced acquaintances who "sympathize" with your marital difficulties and urge you to join them in paradise. (Misery does love company!) Be assured that only a very few singles enjoy the fun-filled life that television portrays, even for short periods of time. Be inclined to take any boasting by single friends with the proverbial grain of salt. And last but not least, be aware that you may be giving up warmth, security, and belonging for whatever adventure and amour you do obtain.

People who believe they can no longer cope with life while married sometimes cope even less well on their own. Singles do go under — lots of them. Make certain that your marital problems are not mainly of your own making, and don't verbalize your divorce intentions unless you are positive — really positive. The words of a threatened divorce are devastating, particularly if they come as a surprise.

It especially is a pity to see so many divorces occur after long-standing marriages because of midlife crisis. The marital breakup of William Loudes and his former wife comes to mind. Months after the divorce he realized: "I was having a kind of second childhood. I was a completely irresponsible person, but if you could see yourself as others see you, you probably wouldn't do half the things you do...I essentially wanted to be single, to see what was on the other side of the fence."

Once a divorce is final, however, it is a waste of time to rehash the past and ponder all the "what if's." The only good reason for looking back is to learn from past mistakes. Could you have made yourself a better, happier mate and persevered? For those of you still married, it is right now, when your marriage is in crisis, that your trauma makes conditions most favorable for taking action to change yourself — and maybe save yourself a lot of grief and misery as well.

When a person's life is proceeding relatively smoothly, or at least proceeding, despite stormy interludes, there is a strong tendency not to seek positive personal change. Only when our emotional pain is great do we normally summon the motivation to seek change and become willing to look at our behavior. If you are suffering in your marriage, this is the time to work on your own negatives and shortcomings. They will certainly follow you out of your marriage and, if substantial, will lead to an unhappy and lonely single life with a succession of unsatisfactory relationships — or maybe no relationships at all.

3.

Eliminate the Negative

Carolyn, a thirty-two year old insurance broker, was quoted in one of the singles magazines as saying, "Before Lou came along, I led a lonely, shallow, and meaningless life... Now my life is just shallow and meaningless."

To most of the recently divorced or widowed, life often does seem bereft of joy and purpose. Of course, even well-adjusted singles and people who are still married occasionally feel the same way. It is simply a fact that some people are better adjusted than others. When misfortune strikes, even though temporarily anxious or depressed, well-adjusted people bounce back quickly. Those who are not so well adjusted are sometimes traumatized into improving themselves and their outlooks; others simply remain unhappy and allow themselves to deteriorate further, often becoming isolated. What happens is largely up to the individual, but remating — often just a desperate attempt to escape loneliness — is never in and of itself the means to make one happy.

MISERY AND COMPANY

It is worth asking why Carolyn still found life meaningless and shallow and, by implication, unhappy after she met Lou and moved in with him. Who was to blame for her continued unhappiness? Lou, for not making her happy? Or herself, because she still harbored negative feelings toward herself and perhaps toward men in general? Might Carolyn's cynical attitude have contributed to or even have caused her divorce? What does her pessimistic outlook say about the quality of her present relationship with Lou? How long can it be expected to last? Is Carolyn fooling herself by thinking that because she is no longer alone she has at least accomplished something and is better off than before? Is she better off?

Only Carolyn has the answers to these questions. Carolyn needs to know where she was, where she is now, and where she hopes to go. She needs to decide if she will need help to achieve the emotional stability necessary to maintain a satisfying long-term relationship. If she has only recently been divorced, the darkened window she views the world through is to be expected. Her world has crashed down around her and she is emotionally devastated. Like physical hurts, blows to the psyche are not only painful but also take time to heal. How much time depends on her emotional state, her decisions, and her actions — and to a certain extent on luck.

Judging from Carolyn's remark, she did not take time to adjust to living alone before moving in with Lou. But what about Lou? Why would he want to enter into a relationship with such an emotionally devastated woman? If Lou is an experienced single, he may have chosen Carolyn because she is attractive, sexy, or wealthy __ or all of these. If he too is newly single and inexperienced, he may have gravitated to her simply to have someone to hold hands with, both physically and psychologically. If Carolyn and Lou are both new-comers to the single life, they would have been better off meeting and dating as many people as possible at this early stage.

On the other hand, let's suppose that both Carolyn and Lou have been single a year or two and remain in their unsatisfactory relationship because they lack confidence in themselves and are afflic-ted with negative feelings they need to work through. You yourself may have been a victim of negative feelings in the past. Take a moment to examine your life. Was it overshadowed by feelings of emptiness and meaninglessness? Did you experience more than the normal amount of anger, guilt, self-pity, resentment, or depression? Most importantly, do you still harbor such negative feelings much of the time? If you do, then action is required to reestablish a reasonably happy emotional climate, and hard work and courage are needed to effect this positive change.

ESCAPING EMOTIONAL DOLDRUMS

Two kinds of action will help us bring about desirable change. First, we can profit from what books and knowledgeable single friends advise: date as often as opportunity permits, make new friends of both sexes, exercise to improve our health, groom to improve our appearance, develop new interests, and participate in some activities — in short, keep busy and get out of the house and out of ourselves. The more difficult effort is to learn something about our own unconscious emotional realities. We have to learn to recognize what we truly feel, and we sometimes need professional help. This is no disgrace, and many singles (and marrieds) do seek help at one time or another.

Let's start with the easier of the two steps, the one designed to help us get out of ourselves and into other people and activities. To be sure, this requires a lot of courage. Here are three of the best things you can do:

1. Attend a divorce or death adjustment seminar.
2. Talk about adjustment problems with an experienced same-sex friend, if you have one, or visit a professional divorce adjustment counselor.
3. Join a singles club and make friends of both sexes.

DIVORCE/DEATH ADJUSTMENT SEMINARS

You may be surprised to learn that most communities have these seminars. They are sponsored by community colleges, churches, or mental health agencies and are usually taught by instructors with degrees in psychology or sociology. Plan to set aside an entire evening every week for three or four months. Although that may sound like a long time, the sessions are so interesting and helpful that the months pass quickly.

During a typical first session the instructor distributes a syllabus describing the subject matter to be covered at each session. It may include a bibliography of books and articles on various aspects of divorce/death adjustment. An annotated bibliography (one with a short synopsis of each book) is the most helpful. A few people in the seminar will probably already have read some of the books and, together with the instructor, may offer some helpful suggestions. Select at least four articles or books in order to familiarize yourself with all of the following topics:

1. Adjusting to the trauma of death or divorce
2. Exploring male sexuality
3. Exploring female sexuality
4. Dating and relating in single life

It's not necessary to read dozens of books on the various subjects. After all, you're not after a Ph.D., only information which will help you adjust to the single lifestyle. Spending too much time at home reading can amount to procrastination — putting off entering the real-life laboratory of dating and relating.

The seminars are typically held in classrooms with the chairs arranged in a semicircle, and usually about ten to twenty people of both sexes will attend. The instructor presides informally and usually opens by briefly describing the psychological and social dynamics of a typical problem facing the newly single. Then most of each session is reserved for discussion.

At first, few people volunteer to speak. Everyone is reluctant to relate their personal feelings and experiences. Competent instructors, however, know how to break the ice, usually by recounting some of their own difficulties with adjustment. They might then ask different people to comment on certain non-threatening aspects of the subject at hand, and the assembled strangers gradually become friendly acquaintances, then friends, and they begin to shed their inhibitions.

It's amazing to see a restrained and inhibited group of people open up and share some of their most intimate feelings. There are times when no one wants to end the discussion; that's when a nearby restaurant often becomes an off-campus classroom and many close friendships are made.

Participants not only learn from each other, but they also draw comfort from the fact that others share the same experiences and feelings. They learn they are not unique in their unhappiness — not the only ones in the world suddenly single and miserable. They begin to understand that they can change things and reclaim a happy frame of mind. Midway through the course, the participants often find themselves laughing (with, not at, each other) over the outrageous slings and arrows that fate has meted out. They have become a cohesive, friendly fellowship.

They strive to help each other. By talking and sharing, they begin to bring about positive changes in their attitudes toward themselves and toward life. Most importantly, they begin to accept the fact that all relationships must ultimately come to an end, and that when they end, a more or less predictable series of events will occur. They learn that pain and negative feelings are inevitable, but that they can cope with those feelings and the pain will pass. Their confidence grows and they realize they will not only survive, but will emerge as stronger and wiser people.

Yes, the most positive outcome of this kind of therapy is the realization that life really does go on after death or divorce. Life continues in a different way, however, and depending on the individual it can be better or worse. Most of us realize that nobody is perfect and will accept part of the responsibility for a marital breakup, but it is more difficult to be entirely honest and raise to the conscious level those negative traits that have hampered our happiness for years. Becoming aware of our shortcomings must be our first step. Without awareness, how can we change? How many times have you said, or heard it said, "She (He) made me do it," or, "For years he (she) insulted me every time we went out." The questions that really need to be asked are, "Why did I do what I didn't want to do?" and "Why did I tolerate such demeaning behavior?" Unless we realize that we allow whatever happens to happen — that we are responsible for ourselves — then we will engage in inappropriate or destructive behavior. Unless we change our attitudes and habits, our ability to relate to others will continue to be flawed. We must become consciously aware of our faults and bad habits, and we must recognize and accept our true feelings.

REMARRIAGE

In a divorce or death adjustment seminar you'll hear a few things you might not want to hear. One of these is "Don't remarry in the first year." I certainly didn't want to hear that. I was among those cut adrift after long marriages, and I wanted to remarry as soon as possible to reestablish the love, warmth, and security that comes with a good or even so-so marriage. Others similarly obsessed find willing collaborators and make one of the biggest mistakes in their lives. But I was plain lucky, not because I didn't sorely want to get married, but because I was unable to find a Ms. Reasonably Right at the time — probably because I myself was in such bad emotional shape as to be Mr. Absolutely Wrong.

Indeed, the reality was that I was in no emotional condition to choose a spouse. It would take a lot of time to work through my emotional trauma. In the ensuing three years, I learned that the instructors were right, that there were many middle-aged men and women trying to remate for inappropriate reasons, and that locating a Mr. or Ms. Reasonably Right is usually difficult, involving lengthy trial and error and then the time to really get to know someone.

One instructor's version of the one-year-wait maxim was: "It's almost never possible to be emotionally prepared to choose wisely and remarry successfully for at least a year after divorce." He went on to relate some of the sad outcomes he had heard about and to point out the statistical evidence of the high failure rate of quick-fix second marriages. He concluded: "You need time to heal and grow, to go out and meet new people, and to engage in new activities. First seek a reasonably satisfactory and happy adjustment to life on your own as a single person. Only then will you have a good chance to relate successfully to a new partner over the long term."

In part because of his advice and in part because I was having difficulty finding the kind of woman I thought I deserved (Loni Anderson would do!), I grudgingly resolved to wait a year before remarrying. My new plan was to get out and around a lot and just plain have a good time before finding someone and settling down —

not exactly a noble plan, but far better than the first one. Also, our instructor supplied us with the names of various Real World and Single World support groups that would help us over the initial rough spots by introducing new interests, new directions, and new friends.

CHURCH AFFILIATION

An especially valuable resource after death or divorce can be your minister, pastor, rabbi, or priest. These people can not only help you gather the spiritual strength to deal with your adversity, but they can also counsel you on practical matters. Many have information about church-sponsored singles groups and can refer you to secular counselors, psychiatrists, and even divorce lawyers.

Some can provide the lion's share of the help you need — maybe even all of it.

Most religious institutions have tended to be almost exclusively family-oriented. That has changed in recent years, and almost all denominations have made large strides in helping the growing numbers of middle-aged singles. However, some people find it difficult to ask a clergyman intimate, personal questions such as "Should I or shouldn't I?" or "Where can I go for a vasectomy?" If you hesitate to ask your clergyman, then ask a divorce adjustment counselor or knowledgeable person in one of the singles groups I've been encouraging you to join.

TRUSTED FRIENDS

Don't overlook getting advice and answers to your questions from trusted single friends and reliable new acquaintances of good reputation in Single World. They can be invaluable in helping you restart your social life. Your married friends won't really be able to comprehend your problems, and, moreover, they tend to drift away. If you already have a trusted and experienced single friend, count yourself among the fortunate few.

If you don't have such friends, you are going to have to make them by joining one or two singles groups. Especially look for friends who share some of your other interests. Making even one friend can have a ripple effect: that friend has friends you can meet, they too have friends, and so on. Before long, you'll find that while you may no longer belong in your old married friends' social circles, you have a new niche for yourself in Single World.

Trusted friends, sometimes referred to as "lifeline friends" in Single World, can not only help you to meet new people, they can also in some instances introduce you to realities about yourself and about self-defeating behaviors you may be unaware of. To be objective about oneself is almost impossible, but a perceptive friend, who is hopefully also kind and tactful, is in a position to tell you things about yourself that may help you effect positive change. Perhaps you're too pessimistic, tearing yourself and others down all the time. You could have an annoying laugh, or be too cynical or inconsiderate. Listening to a list of your shortcomings may not be easy, but ask for a confidential appraisal anyway. It could be very helpful.

PRIVATE ADJUSTMENT COUNSELING

I didn't want to talk about really personal things with the instructor at a divorce adjustment seminar, or with a religious counselor, or with any friend or acquaintance I had at the time. Fortunately, I was able to obtain the names of two competent divorce adjustment counselors, a husband-and-wife team, because I definitely needed to get some one-on-one guidance during those troubled, floundering days.

Private counseling can be very expensive, particularly if you go for a long time. Only you can decide when you have obtained the information you need to get on with your life on your own and with the help of friends and support groups. In my case, we had weekly meetings for about three months. I was helped to perceive the self-defeating dating practices I pursued — pursued with unsuitable and equally floundering partners. Moreover, I received excellent practical advice about where to meet new people and develop new interests, both in Real World and in Single World. Finally, I got some good answers to delicate questions I had concerning dating and relating practices.

Divorce and death adjustment counselors can be found in most communities, and not all of them are expensive. Some excellent counselors are sponsored by churches and by community and family service organizations and are available at nominal cost. The best way to find a good counselor is by referrals from friends or acquaintances who have been well served. Your clergyman also may be of help with a referral, or maybe a knowledgeable friend in one of the singles clubs can help.

SEX IN SINGLE WORLD

For me, sex in Single World constituted something new and threatening. Like many other men, I was fearful of potential dysfunction — a fear which prompted me to prove over and over again that I was okay. To be sure, had I continued testing my virility long enough, I surely would have had problems. I had good reason to be pleased that my counseling team had been trained in sex therapy. They guided me to a less frantic, more enjoyable approach, while helping me to achieve better attitudes toward sex, women, and myself.

One of my questions was, "How important is sex to middle-aged people?" I learned that many, perhaps most, mature adults enjoy active sex lives into their fifties, sixties, and beyond — sometimes way beyond. Phil Donahue taped a show in Miami where very elderly adults freely admitted to continuing sexual enjoyment. The old saying "If you don't use it, you'll lose it" applies as much to sex as to anything else.

Those with good attitudes know that the key to good sex in middle life is adjusting to physical change as we get older and utilizing compensating techniques. *Forbes* magazine quoted Dr. Helen Kaplan, Director of the Human Sexuality Teaching Program at the New York Hospital Cornell Medical Center, as saying, "Fortunately, sexuality is among the last functions to fall prey to the aging process."

PSYCHOLOGICAL/PSYCHIATRIC COUNSELING

Painful anxiety attacks or deep depression often dog the footsteps of the newly widowed or divorced. Here, too, a death or divorce adjustment counselor can be helpful. In some cases, however, the symptoms are so severe that the services of a psychiatrist or psychologist are called for. Anxiety and depression are experienced to some degree by almost every newly single person. However, some experience such great emotional pain that they actually think they're going crazy. In my research were numerous examples of suddenly divorced or bereaved middle-aged men and women who contemplated suicide. Others became stuck in the past. Many became obsessed with the "what if's" and "whose fault's" and compulsively relived the distressing histories of their former marriages.

My research also revealed that the majority of divorced people thought their marital breakups were primarily the faults of their former spouses. My perception was that, like myself, they too might have contributed greatly. Coming from different backgrounds, having different values, and growing at different speeds can all contribute to a marital breakup, but so can the shortcomings of both partners. In any event, now is a good time to deal with any useless emotional baggage you might have carried around for years. From that standpoint alone, it may be desirable to consult a qualified, well-recommended mental health professional.

Exhaustive studies have shown that at any given time a substantial percentage of adult Americans suffers to some extent from mild neuroses or compulsions. Anxiety, phobias, panic disorders, and depression need not be serious to take the joy out of living. Moreover, alcohol and drug abuse cause widespread suffering and devastate countless lives. Surprisingly, fewer than one in five people who suffer from any of these problems seeks professional help.

Although a qualified mental health professional can help, not all licensed professionals are equally competent. It's wise to seek out recommendations from people you know and trust. One of your goals in treatment should be to gain insight into your unconscious negative thinking patterns which cause pain, worry, and anguish. These symptoms, together with their underlying causes, interfere with your entering and maintaining a committed, loving relationship. A good therapist or counselor will help you recognize these tendencies, but eliminating them is your responsibility.

Anger and resentment were the foremost negative traits among the divorced women I dated. I dated women who were so deeply involved emotionally in their love-hate feelings for their ex-husbands that they had absolutely nothing to contribute to a new relationship. Sometimes I got the impression that their anger predated their divorces and contributed to their marital failures. Feelings of guilt for leaving a spouse or self-pity for being left are other negatives which swallow single people in emotional quicksand.

The sooner negative emotions can be brought to the surface, identified, labeled, and dealt with, the better. They keep you from being pleasant company on a date and from sustaining a relationship long enough to relate on a meaningful level. To hear a litany of miseries from a newly divorced or newly widowed person is not uncommon; in fact, it's to be expected. But in time such lamentations become boring and turn people away.

In some cases you can recognize and seek to deal with emotional negatives more or less on your own by introspection — introspection nourished by reading appropriate books and articles and listening to what your lifeline friends have to say about you. Too much introspection, of course, can be self-defeating. A good idea is to actually schedule an hour or so every other day when you permit yourself to introspect — and to worry about things. You can begin by asking yourself if you are predisposed to be angry at the opposite sex because of childhood experiences, or are one of those people who expect the worst (and usually get it) by repeatedly inviting rejection.

If you look back on your broken marriage, do so only to learn more about yourself. Never mind your former spouse's faults — that's his or her problem now. You're out to help yourself. What were your own negative emotions and deeds? Have you improved? To be sure, bringing negatives to the surface is difficult; we tend to deny their existence. And even after you do recognize them, and recognize how they trigger self-defeating behavior, you will still need time to internalize the knowledge of them in your heart and mind. There's that nasty word again: time. Once more we are reminded that there are few quick fixes.

A valuable point is made in *Games People Play* by Dr. Eric Berne. We are told that many of us must change the negative "tapes" we carry around unbeknownst in our heads. These tapes, often dating from childhood, cause us to act automatically in inappropriate, negative ways. An example of this negative programming is telling yourself over and over that you are no good, perhaps because you were repeatedly told so as a child. If you listen to that internal tape daily, you accept the fact that you are no good and act accordingly. However, if you change the tape to say that the record really shows you to be a worthwhile person, then you begin to accept these positive affirmations. In time you will unconsciously heed the new tape instead of the old one, and you will act accordingly. This retaping takes conscious effort, energy, and time. But it can be done — many have done it. Once we erase some of the negatives and replace them with positives, better relationships inevitably follow.

While you are working to improve yourself in this manner, show yourself a little kindness and tolerance. Realize that most emotional shortcomings are part of the human condition. Unfortunately, when we think in terms of what is "normal" and "sane," we too often think of people who seem to be exceptionally well adjusted — like we perhaps think we ought to be. That is, we erroneously equate "normalcy" with the Ozzies and Harriets of this world. When we feel we are going crazy, the reality most of the time is that we are simply experiencing psychic pain, which will pass in time.

GOING CRAZY?

Every once in a while you may bump into someone who suffers from a truly severe and chronic mental illness — as opposed to the garden-variety neuroses many of us suffer. This is rare; the "system" usually puts such unfortunates out on the street, where readers of this book will seldom see them, or in prisons or mental institutions. If you encounter such a person, you'll quickly learn what "crazy" really means. A friend was asked by a woman suffering from deep depression and anguish if he thought she sounded like she was going crazy. He replied, "No. If you were, you wouldn't be asking about it." Certainly this is not a guaranteed acid test for craziness, but you get the idea.

On the other hand, if you do feel intense anxiety, guilt, or depression over a long period of time, by all means seek professional help. As I pointed out, this can be valuable if for no other reason than that it affords the opportunity to gain insights into your negative traits, and we all have some neurotic feelings we could part with. The vast majority of times, we will be assured that our mental anguish is just that, and not the onset of true mental illness.

ALCOHOL, DRUG, AND FOOD ABUSE

While people who are anxious about the possibility of going insane seldom do go insane, those who are concerned about the possibility that they are becoming addicted to alcohol or other drugs really have something to worry about. The compulsion to overeat, that is, food addiction, is related, as are other eating disorders such as anorexia and bulimia. Addiction sneaks up slowly and insidiously, and denial plays a major role in development of the problem. The afflicted person doesn't see the problem for what it really is — an addiction. Be on guard when you hear, or find yourself saying, "I can stop whenever I really want to." Denial works overtime to keep the victim from seeking help. Instead, the addiction worsens until the victim finally has no choice but to get help or suffer dire consequences.

Only very rarely can people stop drinking or taking drugs permanently on their own, and even more rarely do they find peace of mind in solitary abstinence. Here, too, professionals can be of great help, particularly in early recovery, but the vast majority of successfully recovering addicts find continuing help in fellowship with other recovering sufferers. Alcoholics Anonymous (AA), Narcotics Anonymous (NA), and Overeaters Anonymous (OA) cannot be praised too highly.

Studies have shown that while one drink a day may even be healthful to non-alcoholics, more than that usually produces a number of negative results. Imperceptibly, over a period of time, some people progress from social drinking, where they can truly take it or leave it, to dependence and chronic drunkenness. The scenarios for drug and food addictions are similar. The person is indeed rare who has not seen the effects of an addiction on someone close to them, but it is sometimes very difficult to accept our own addictions.

DRINKING, DRUG TAKING, AND SOCIALIZING

Society has come to rely inordinately on alcohol and other drugs to act as social lubricants. Singles functions are far from an exception. Tension is involved in meeting and dating members of the opposite sex; participating in singles activities is somewhat stress-producing even for the veteran. A drink or two can serve as a social relaxant, but this behavior is far different from that of the pre-alcoholic who needs to drink to cope or the full-blown alcoholic who needs to drink, period.

Some alcoholics are hard to identify because they don't consume large quantities. It's what alcohol does to you, not how much you drink. Most alcoholics, however, are heavy drinkers. Most of these are called "functional alcoholics" because they continue to hold jobs, albeit at reduced efficiency. Middle-class alcoholics are often protected by friends, family, money, and/or social or professional position. One does not have to be a drunken skid-row bum to be an alcoholic. Many die en route from suicide or accidents; many are imprisoned or institutionalized. Fortunately, many recover.

To date someone with an ongoing addiction is a serious mistake, and to enter into a relationship is usually devastating. Addictions are a constant source of mental problems, illness, dishonesty, bad decisions, the inability to relate to others, and, of course, crime. The compulsive behavior is often just a symptom of character and personality flaws.

We need to be aware that drug addicts include those who are hooked on prescription drugs as well as those using illicit drugs. Unfortunately, some physicians whip out their prescription pads at the drop of a patient's hint and write ever-increasing dosages. You can be positive the trouble is serious if someone has to visit two or more doctors to obtain enough mood-altering drugs. While the drug of choice of middle-aged men is usually alcohol, middle-aged women will frequently abuse prescription drugs — or food!

If you go on a first date with someone who drinks too much or gives evidence of abusing drugs, whether he or she behaves badly or not, it's a good idea to stop and consider if you should make the first date serve as the last one as well. If your date uses illicit drugs, run do not walk to the nearest exit.

If you think that you yourself may possibly be abusing alcohol or drugs, you probably are. "If it looks like a duck, walks like a duck, and quacks like a duck, it's probably a duck." Seek help from one of the recovery fellowships.

RECOVERY FELLOWSHIPS

The most successful program helping people to overcome alcoholism, and certainly the least expensive, is Alcoholics Anonymous. Parallel noncommercial programs patterned after AA, and also enjoying success, include the already-mentioned Narcotics Anonymous and

Overeaters Anonymous groups, as well as Gamblers Anonymous, Cocaine Anonymous, Emotions Anonymous, Smokers Anonymous, and probably others. While perhaps not as speedily destructive as alcohol or drug abuse, compulsive overeating, compulsive gambling, compulsive neurotic behavior, and certainly smoking exact their own tolls of suffering.

Many other nonprofit and for-profit programs are designed to help people along these lines. There is Recovery Inc. for emotional problems, for example, and Weight Watchers, Nutri System, Cambridge, and a host of other weight-control programs. However, the minimal cost of the anonymous programs plus the excellent results many achieve in them make them worthy of an earnest first look. AA and the others are financed by small voluntary donations from the members — by passing the hat at meetings. There are no dues or fees to lighten the often-depleted pocketbooks of divorced and widowed individuals.

The anonymous fellowships enjoy great success for at least two underlying reasons. First, they provide social support networks and friendship circles for people afflicted by common problems. Second, the group discussions, which usually take up most of the meeting times, constitute effective group therapy — as well as an educational forum. Members typically improve their lives dramatically — emotionally, socially, economically, physically, and spiritually. Newcomers can meet and get to know as friends the veteran members who have successfully dealt with their addictions and gone on to lead satisfying, happy, and successful lives. Neophytes come to realize that there is a very good chance they can do the same.

Generally, two kinds of meetings are held by the anonymous programs. The speakers' meeting consists of one or two people getting up and telling their personal stories and sharing their experiences, strength, and hope. Listeners often find themselves relating to the experiences of a speaker; they are able to discern similar shortcomings in themselves and learn how the speaker achieved progress. Speakers' meetings are usually open to the general public.

The second kind of meeting is the discussion meeting, often closed to nonmembers to help preserve the members' anonymity. Here the participants exchange opinions, feelings, approaches, and suggestions concerning a topic related to their addiction and recovery. The result is a better understanding of themselves and of others.

Each of the anonymous programs welcomes newly divorced and widowed people. To join, all you have to do is show up at a meeting and express a desire to become a member. You use only your first name, and you're not hassled about your drinking, drug taking, overeating, gambling, or whatever. All the excuses you've used for your destructive behavior are familiar to the members, who used them themselves. They know what you're going through because they've been there. They support your efforts, and as long as you are willing, they will be there to help. If you stop attending meetings nobody will come after you and try to get you to come back. If you do return, having sunk even lower into your addiction, you will be welcomed back — for as many times as it takes.

Aside from providing excellent environments in which to overcome compulsions, the anonymous programs offer still another advantage. The time spent in meetings means less time spent at home in painful introspection leading nowhere. Instead, you are making new friends who will point the way to somewhere — and enjoying great fellowship in the process.

COMPULSIVE OVEREATING

More and more time, money, and attention is being devoted to the serious problem of overeating. Indeed, obesity does get in the way of successfully dating, relating, and remating. Like alcoholics, compulsive overeaters can and do use the unconscious mechanism of denial. On one mental level they deny to themselves that they are too fat, though on another level they fully realize the extent of their affliction and the costs they are paying in terms of health and social life. We're not talking about ten or twenty pounds of extra weight that might turn only a few people off; it's the thirty, forty, fifty, or a hundred excess pounds that almost inevitably will chill romance with desirable dates. Right or wrong, fair or not, people who are markedly overweight are at a definite disadvantage in the mating game.

Next to eating less, the most important part of any weight loss program is regular exercise. Not only will you burn off fat, develop muscle tone, and hence look better, you will feel better — sometimes much better. Scientists have only recently discovered that this sense of well-being that comes from exercise is not just a heightened sense of accomplishment. Subtle brain chemistry is involved. Exercise has been shown to be effective against even severe depression and anxiety. Think of how it can help you through your occasional blues and anxious evenings alone. You don't have to run marathons or pump iron. Walking, swimming, and bicycling are all excellent exercises — and let's certainly not forget dancing.

TESTING FOR AN ALCOHOL OR DRUG PROBLEM

If you think you have, or possibly might have, a problem with alcohol or drugs — or both — or if your family, acquaintances, doctor, lawyer, or minister tells you that you might have a problem; or if society has punished you because of something you did under the influence; then it's time to join and become active in Alcoholics Anonymous or Narcotics Anonymous. You can always quit if you are not addicted. If you are addicted, then you will have made the best decision of your life.

A simple test can help people determine for themselves whether or not they have an alcohol problem: Buy two liters of your favorite liquor (68 ounces). Drink two ounces every day (or two cans of beer or two six-ounce glasses of wine), but only two, and don't skip any days. Do this until both bottles are empty, which should take a little over a month. Needless to say, don't drink anything alcoholic except from this supply. If you can stick to this schedule for two months, regardless of the good and bad events in your life, the celebrations and crises that come up, then you are in good shape — probably only a social drinker. But if you cannot stick to your schedule for the entire two months, if you finish the bottles ahead of time, then you would do well to try AA. And watch out for "denial." One man finished his two bottles in three days but denied that the test was fair because his pet had died. The next two bottles took him a whole week, so he figured he was on the way to having his problem licked.

A simple way to help determine if you are abusing prescription drugs is also to precisely control your intake for two months. Take your prescriptions exactly as directed, never more or less and only at the proper times. Needless to say, don't take any other drugs or drink alcohol during those two months, and we're talking about the prescriptions from only one doctor.

Only after you seek to eliminate or minimize the kinds of negatives described in this chapter can you successfully accentuate your positives and grow into a more interesting, more desirable, and more dateable you. In the next chapter we'll show you some of the options available to help you do just that.

4.

Accentuate the Positive

Frustrated by my early difficulties in finding women to date, I asked an experienced single, "Where in the world do you meet people?" His reply: "Wherever people are." I thought he was too flippant and insensitive about a problem that was truly exasperating and bothering me, but technically he was right. You can meet people everywhere. However, saying hello to someone standing in the checkout line at a supermarket rarely leads to a date; more often it results in another rejection you certainly don't need.

While it may be true that you can meet people everywhere, not every place in Real World is conducive to giving or receiving invitations for dates. You might both be vibrant and attractive, but in Real World it's still difficult to arrange a date with a stranger who hasn't been introduced by a friend. That isn't to say it can't happen; but only in Casual World, with its associated risks, can you quickly and effortlessly get together with strangers.

Singles clubs (and singles travel groups) do provide a popular middle ground, which helps the sexes quickly get acquainted, and they do provide at least some opportunity for people to learn a little about potential dates by observing them over time and asking friends or acquaintances about them. However, singles clubs are not as productive as many would like in helping them find Mr. or Ms. Reasonably Right to ride off into the sunset with.

REAL WORLD REVISITED

Your chances of finding Mr. or Ms. Reasonably Right are best — although it might take months or even years — when you get involved in some of the myriad interests and activities pursued by the population at large: church groups, political organizations, sports teams, exercise and health clubs, investment seminars, nature and conservation groups, library groups, film clubs, recovery fellowships, adult education classes, bridge clubs, college classes, hobby clubs, civic groups — the list is endless. Newspapers and local magazines list dozens of clubs and activities, classes and seminars.

Bulletin boards in libraries, churches, colleges, and government buildings are good sources too. Once you start looking, you'll be amazed by all that goes on in Real World.

By all means continue your current Real World interests while you develop new ones, even though at times it will be necessary to transfer those interests to new social circles. Husband-and-wife bridge clubs, for example, are obviously not for you.

In contrast to the singles clubs, where eager hopefuls often find themselves making the rounds as fast as they can, Real World allows time — lots of it — for the sexes to really get to know each other and share friends and interests before they draw close to one another. In contrast, singles club members often share only one common interest — finding someone — and members may have little other than the social scene to talk about. Nevertheless, you should join a singles club early on in order to get out of the house, get out of yourself, and get some practice dating and dealing with the opposite sex. But realize that perhaps only one out of a hundred Single World dates ends in either successful relating and/or remating.

TAKE A DEEP BREATH AND BEGIN

It takes courage to join new groups, and it also takes self-imposed discipline to participate regularly and dependably, especially in the beginning when you may not know anyone. You'll naturally feel nervous and uncomfortable, but with a little effort you'll soon make new friends. Think of it this way: Any activity, project, or interest you pursue in order to round out your life or improve your health will inevitably create opportunities for meeting new friends to replace some of the old ones who drift away. Add a little luck and some of those friends will turn into dates.

Make a special effort to seek out entirely new activities. How about taking an adult education course in art? A friend points to one woman who thought she had absolutely no talent but wanted to know something about watercolors. "If nothing else, I'll be able to appreciate art more after the classes," she said. While she's not another Rembrandt, she has become an accomplished painter, has spent many pleasurable hours at her easel, and has been accepted into the social circles of local artists and art enthusiasts.

Almost any new activity will help you to ease out of your single-hood trauma. Empty hours which might otherwise be wasted in painful introspection and sadness are now filled with structure and purpose. Restoration of self-esteem and a general feeling of well-being will soon follow. As your horizons broaden and your outlook brightens, you become happier, more interesting, and more attractive.

Relationships in Real World evolve over time, and therefore most of the screening of potential dates to evaluate their personalities and character is accomplished unconsciously and automatically. Chances are that one shared interest, such as teaching Sunday school, is representative of an entire constellation of shared interests and values. The hit or miss — usually miss — of trial-and-error Single World dating is eliminated. Instead, you get to know each other and are drawn together in a comfortable, unselfconscious way.

REAL WORLD PURSUITS

What specific kinds of Real World interests and activities are we talking about? For convenience, these can be divided into four categories: (1) sports and exercise, (2) the sciences and business, (3) cultural arts and crafts, and (4) miscellaneous, including religion, politics, charities, and self-help. Many pursuits belong to more than one of these categories, and within each of these are literally hundreds of options to choose from.

A word about time. Some people claim they absolutely do not have time to pursue any leisure interests or activities. For some this may almost be literally true and, if so, very sad. Financially pinched working mothers with children still at home sometimes come close, but there are still things they can do. Remember, it's a matter of priorities; people find the time to do the things they want to do. We sometimes just have to change what we want to do. We can lie down and mope or stand up and do calisthenics, watch ho-hum TV sitcoms or take a course in writing comedy, swap lies with cronies in a dim bar or go to a singles club rap, sweep the rug we swept yesterday or take a class in weaving rugs, grouse on the phone about politics or go to a rally.

I suggest that everyone pick out at least one social activity from each of the four categories. Anticipate that weeks may go by before you feel really comfortable with your new pursuits and relaxed in the social situations they entail. Obviously you cannot be active in each of your four groups every night, but you should attend them regularly and dependably. Soon your new friends will miss you and ask after you when you are unavoidably absent. Focus on the intrinsic value of each activity; the payoff in dating will come in due time. Your interim dating will be taken care of by your fifth category of activity — your singles groups.

Activities for middle-agers depend more on individual preference than on chronological age. This period of life is very elastic and can be extended by good physical and mental health. A dictionary may say middle age is from about forty to sixty, but we've all met seemingly elderly people in their thirties and vibrant, ageless men and women in their seventies and eighties. As many people say, "Age is only a number." What we think, what we feel, and especially what we do will determine the extent of our enjoyment of the ever-lengthening period of middle life.

A HEALTHIER YOU

Good physical health is especially important to us during the crisis that follows divorce or death of a spouse. To be sure, good health is important to anyone aspiring for a place in the winner's circle of life, regardless of marital status, but during survival coping, health becomes important as never before because of its close ties to mental well-being and physical attractiveness. When you're "too tired" to exercise, do so anyway. Unless you're ill, force yourself to stick to whatever exercise plan you devised. There have been countless times when I absolutely, positively did not want to do my exercises but griped and grunted my way through them anyway. Every time, I felt much better for having done them — every single time. I have almost never gone for a walk, or a bicycle ride, or a swim, and not come home feeling better.

I recall reading about a man who was always tired. He didn't think of himself as depressed, "...just no zest for living," he'd say. His doctor told him to get some exercise, but he objected, "I'm too tired," and his life dragged on. Then one day he finally decided to give it a try. Every night he dragged his exhausted body out of the house to the overgrown, scrubby acreage behind his garage and chopped away at the dead trees and underbrush that clogged his property. At first he could work for only a few minutes at a time, but as the weeks went by his strength increased. After a few months, when the project was completed, he was amazed to realize he had regained his old energy, and he couldn't help but notice how much happier he felt.

The satisfaction resulting from regular exercise lifts the spirits and at the same time raises one's self-esteem and self-confidence. Like everything else in a death/divorce recovery program, results do take time. To be sure, it may take a good while to get really fit and reach your goals, but you will start feeling and looking better as soon as you start. There also is comfort and solace in knowing that although it may take a long time — perhaps two or three years — to reach your health goals, you will surely get there if you keep plugging.

Begin with a thorough physical examination. Your doctor will tell you if there are any restrictions. If you intend to lose weight, particularly a lot of weight, get some diet guidelines and a realistic time frame from your doctor or another professional. Join Overeaters Anonymous, Weight Watchers, or a similar group. These support groups have much better track records than any of the proliferating miracle diets, which, as you know, account for one of the biggest chunks of the publishing industry.

What kind of exercise? Aerobics is best for weight loss, muscle tone, heart and lung capacity, your complexion, and your feeling of well-being. All aerobics basically amounts to is doing something repetitive that increases your heart rate and makes you breathe somewhat more heavily for at least twenty minutes. You can join an aerobics workout club, or you can exercise at home with a Jane Fonda video or similar tape, though many people get bored of doing this.

Some sports are obviously better aerobically than others, for example, running or jogging, but these may be too rigorous early in your program, or simply not your cup of tea. But how about swimming or bicycling? It takes real ingenuity to turn some other sports, golf for example, into a good workout, but you can do it. Make it a point to walk as fast as you can between every second lie. Just about anything that involves physical effort can, with a little ingenuity, be made into an exercise. One of the best all-around exercises is walking. Next time you drive to the supermarket, park your car a little farther away from the store. Better yet, go to the mall and walk briskly for half an hour. Another outstanding, but seldom touted, healthful exercise is stretching, one of the best all-around things you can do for your body.

Try to stretch your budget, too, and join one of the coed health clubs, or spas as they are sometimes called. They have become very popular meeting grounds for singles and, though sometimes moderately costly, are far cheaper in the long run than singles bars. The instructors can help you establish goals and set up an exercise program tailored to your needs. The facilities usually include all kinds of exercise equipment, a pool, sauna, and a steam room. Some are open twenty-four hours.

If you're having trouble deciding on a sports/exercise program, then you might consider the following three questions:

1. Which sports or exercise programs do I think I might enjoy the most — or hate the least?

2. Which programs attract the kinds of participants I'd like to meet?

3. How can I find ways to afford the time and expense?

I started a diet and exercise program almost immediately after my divorce, somehow feeling that my very survival was at stake. I swam, walked, or biked in nice weather and used an exercise bicycle in foul weather. I joined a weekend bicycling group which not only provided excellent exercise but became an important part of my social life and a good source for dates. (The women in the group found even more dates.) I exercised faithfully enough to manage to lose weight, tone up, and vent some anger and frustration.

In my early fifties at the time, I set out to lose twenty to thirty pounds of excess fat and started a diet, which I interrupted with a food binge now and then. If your experience is similar to mine, your waistline, at least, will benefit from the emotional turmoil of divorce. You lose pounds almost effortlessly for a while, but months later when you start feeling better your appetite returns and the fat you lost fights its way back. The price you must pay for freedom from being overweight is the same as you must pay for political liberty and professional or social success: eternal vigilance.

Cutting back on alcohol is a good way to lose weight; alcohol has almost as many calories as pure lard. Say you eliminate two drinks before dinner, each containing about 150 calories. That's 300 a day, 2100 a week, and a little over 109,000 calories a year. Divide that by the approximate 3500 calories it takes to make a pound of fat, and you have thirty-one pounds. One drink a day amounts to fifteen pounds a year.

Even worse, drinks before meals always sharpened my appetite and reduced my willpower to resist the temptation to overeat. I quit drinking altogether, read up on what constituted a good diet, and proceeded to eat — most of the time — easy to prepare, low calorie, nutritious meals. I began to eat a lot of raw fruits and vegetables and microwave dinners like Lean Cuisine and Weight Watchers.

Incidentally, I soon gave up an earlier notion of learning to become a good cook. Eating alone was never fun for me anyway, so why cook? Many women I dated, some of them excellent cooks, confided that they seldom cooked for themselves, at least not the way they used to cook, and for the same reason.

A SMARTER YOU

One way thousands of singles have developed new interests, learned new skills, and made new friends is by becoming students again. This does not necessarily involve a big commitment on your part; you don't have to take courses for credit or work toward a degree or certification. Junior colleges, as well as many universities, offer dozens of inexpensive, non-credit "continuing education" or "adult education" classes. Sometimes it is also possible to audit regular college courses without earning credit or having to take the tests. Many high schools, libraries, museums, civic centers, civic leagues, foundations, YMCA's, YWCA's, hospitals, and even civic-minded corporations also offer classes. The fact is, you'd be hard pressed to think of some art, science, hobby, craft, sport, or trade you can't find a class in somewhere.

Many new singles reassess their career goals and do go back to school for credit. Many who had quit high school or college in midstream go back to get their diplomas or degrees. Many go to trade schools. In particular, many women who have not been in the work force for years take courses in real estate, travel agency work, and the like. Junior colleges have a special appeal to those who need specialized training or would just like a little more education but have no need for a four-year degree. Always remember that you don't have to stick with an educational goal just because you started it. College freshmen aren't usually expected to know what they will eventually major in. Why should you be any different? Enjoy yourself. Far too many new singles push themselves to the breaking point trying to build new careers overnight.

Continuing education classes are usually open to anybody who wants to attend, and they are especially favored by middle-aged singles. Inexpensive and not overly demanding of one's time, they provide instruction in such diverse subjects as cake decorating, auto mechanics, art appreciation, bookkeeping, child care, gourmet cooking, computer programming, dog obedience, fishing, typing, floral arranging, foreign languages, calligraphy, taxes, jewelry making, guitar playing, photography, amateur astronomy, ecology, oil painting, sewing, psychology, public speaking, and creative writing. Last but certainly not least are the already mentioned classes and seminars on death/divorce adjustment and the other classes of particular interest to singles such as life management, stress management, interpersonal skills, personal finance, and self image. One or two of these classes should be on your "must" list.

Consider giving preference to a few offerings which will be largely populated by the opposite sex. A man might take gourmet cooking, art appreciation, self-assertiveness training, yoga, or even knitting. A woman could take investments, wood carving, public speaking, or even auto mechanics. While you are in and around the classroom maintain an open and receptive attitude. If things seem right, exercise a little initiative in getting to know people who interest you.

If there's a community college or university near you, go by and pick up all the course catalogs and related pamphlets you can lay your hands on. Pick up a copy of the college newspaper, too.

Then spend an hour or so just wandering around. Drop by the coffee shop, the library, and the bookstore. Make it a point to stop at every bulletin board you see, look it over, and take notes. Later, look over all the material you picked up and make your decisions. Your next stop may be the admissions office.

My own post-divorce experiences in adult education began with a divorce adjustment seminar at a local junior college. Later I enrolled in a few more evening classes including Interpersonal Relationships and Assertiveness Training. I enrolled in these two on the recommendation of another bachelor who told me, "That's where the women are." He was right. However, art and music appreciation courses I later took were much more beneficial for me because they constituted a foundation for my subsequent forays into the cultural world of art, music, and theater — a world I had always neglected.

There are frequent new twists in the singles education arena. One example was The Learning Annex in New York. Bill Zanker, its founder, describes what is offered as follows: "You learn something, it's entertaining, and an entire course lasts two hours." *Forbes* reported that optimistic investors see The Learning Annex as a budget-priced alternative to Club Med and singles bars. A promotional blurb reads: "The Learning Annex includes a monthly magazine listing hundreds of activities and courses designed to make friends, have fun, and also learn something." Sacramento has a similar program called the Learning Exchange.

You can also become "a smarter you" by reading books, and you can meet people if you do some of that reading in your local public or college library, especially if you regularly go on the same days at the same times. While you're at it, be on the alert for library-sponsored films, seminars, and special events. Go one step further by joining the Friends of the Library group, if one exists, and you'll open a lot of doors.

A MORE INTERESTING YOU

The crisis of single-shock opens up many possibilities for change and growth. I made a conscious effort to change everything about my life, including my attitude toward cultural activities. I was willing to force myself to try anything, even overcome my fear of the people who were "cultured." I had considered cultural activities to be nebulous, expensive, time-consuming, and frivolous. I used to think that only rich, idle, overeducated people could afford to participate and were equipped to appreciate (if they really did) serious art, classical music, opera, ballet, classical theater, and the like. Now I know that you don't have to be rich to enjoy beautiful art and music and that some of the poorest people have a deep appreciation for culture.

Dictionaries define culture as the development, improvement, or refinement of the mind, emotions, interests, manners, or tastes. The verb form pertains to biology or agriculture and means to grow. I decided to grow, and I began by attending a few plays, concerts, and ballets. Those early evenings were diverting, though not an instant hit with me, and a lot better than sitting home alone feeling awful. Next, I met someone who was going to try out for a bit part in a community playhouse production of Steve Allen's farce, *Don't Drink the Water*, and I was invited to try out too.

I had absolutely no theater experience, not even as an extra, but much to my surprise I landed a small part as a servant. The group experienced difficulty getting organized to rehearse. Infighting and disharmony soon led to the play's falling behind schedule, and with opening night only a month away, some of the key players had yet to memorize their parts. I had at least memorized my few lines (every now and then I was supposed to pop onto the stage and say something profound like, "Sir, the Sultan has arrived"), but I was extremely nervous about performing live and dreaded the prospect of opening night. Fortunately, events intervened to spare both me and the audience.

The director quit and there was a complete shake-up of the cast and other personnel. The new producer-director laid down the law: "Rehearsals will be every night for the next three weeks. If anyone is not able to be here every night, let me know here and now and you will be replaced." These words were music to my ears, and the man would be my friend for life. I had in fact made other commitments and could withdraw in good conscience. My career as an actor had ended before it began (thank goodness!), but I'm glad I had the experience. The brave new world of theater was exciting, if nothing else.

About that time I also decided to try to develop a liking for classical music. I wanted to meet and get to know the kind of people who regularly attend concerts and other cultural events, and I also really wanted to learn to appreciate classical music. In those early post-divorce days it was distressing for me to listen to the romantic ballads and show tunes my wife and I had enjoyed throughout our long marriage, and the easy listening stations on my stereo evoked only painful nostalgia for the "good old days." Switching stations, I found hard rock too frantic, disco too repetitious and uninteresting, and country and western too melancholy. That left classical music, which I resolved to tune in continuously until it became familiar and

I learned to enjoy it. I took an adult education course in music appreciation and started attending concerts. I still occasionally go to concerts, but I have become familiar with most of the better known classics by listening to them on the radio. Indeed, classical music is becoming a source of ever-increasing enjoyment for me.

Perhaps I deserved only a "D" for my efforts in theater and maybe a "C" for music appreciation, but I really earned an "A" for my efforts in the world of art. Several months after taking a course in art appreciation, I learned that the world's largest collection of Salvador Dali's art works was being transferred to this area and that volunteers would be trained as docents (museum tour guides). An acquaintance convinced me to sign up for the museum's training program on Dali and surrealism.

At first, I felt intimidated because most of the others in the program seemed to possess a vast knowledge of art. By this time, however, I had learned that if I refrained from saying anything about my ignorance, nobody would notice. We were given excellent instruction, I really applied myself, and in time I was among those people looked up to for knowing a lot about Dali — and I did! I made many friends in the training program and was elected president of the class alumni group. And I had been so fearful of not being accepted! I became an active docent and conducted tours for three years. I loved the atmosphere of the museum, and many social opportunities were opened up for me — all for the slight cost of forcing myself out of the house and into new interests.

A MORE ACTIVE YOU

In the process of surveying Real World for activities and interests, I found many opportunities I had previously ignored. I attended an Annual International Food Fair, for example, where people in the community from different ethnic groups came together to celebrate their heritage with crafts exhibits, music, and ethnic dances, and, of course, delicious food from diverse cultures. Most communities boast any number of literary groups, historical societies, patriotic organizations, and civic clubs. Who is to say that your Mr. or Ms. Reasonably Right doesn't belong to some group you forced yourself to join? The key word here is join. You might say, "I've been to the museum a dozen times and never met a soul," or, "I've been to every football game since the franchise came to town and never spoken more than five words to anybody." Well, how about meetings sponsored by the museum? Look on the bulletin board. How about football booster clubs? Call the team office.

We are not limited only to our leisure hours in pursuing a better life. Much more than we tend to realize, our work provides structure and purpose — and the need to fill hours of the day outside of ourselves. This is especially important to the suddenly single.

My own experiences certainly brought home to me the benefits to be gained from working. My lifelong notion had been that we work so that we can obtain the financial wherewithal to retire young. I had accomplished this. However, like Carolyn in the last chapter, I found that my life had become largely empty and meaningless. The idleness and aimlessness of simply marking time in retirement fostered bad habits and a bad attitude, both of which contributed to my share in causing the divorce. I then not only had nothing to do, but nobody to do it with.

Finding suitable work was not an easy task, and at first I had to settle for volunteer work. Next I found a part-time job, and it was quite a while before I began to work full-time. If you must, begin the way I did. Anyone can find volunteer work, even if it consists of half a day once a week as a hospital or Red Cross volunteer, but keep looking for a suitable full-time job. It doesn't have to be your ideal job, just one to keep you occupied.

Your workplace can be a good source of dates, especially if you work around many people of the opposite sex. Though there is a good case against getting involved in office romances, I have generally found that more is lost by cautious inaction — often a surrender to fear — than by intelligent risk taking.

What about meeting possible dating partners and new friends at the various places people regularly go to take care of necessary chores? Is it a good idea to wear an open, sunny smile and invite possible approaches when you go the supermarket, the bank, the laundromat, or a shopping mall?

During my early efforts to find dates I tried this, but I had little success. Feeling low and wearing a sunny smile was hard for me, and I had not recovered sufficient emotional balance to risk rejection. Accordingly, I found it extremely difficult to ask women at the vegetable bins about cooking artichokes, let alone to concoct an original pickup approach. While some others can no doubt initiate liaisons in this manner, the technique was not worth the emotional cost to me, and I soon learned that there were much easier ways for me to meet people. I'm referring to Single World, the world of singles clubs and singles travel I'll describe next, in Part II.

5.

Here I Go Again

To most married people, Single World is a mysterious, suspect, hedonistic subculture, and the newcomer often finds this uncharted territory at once enticing and scary. To be sure, there are pitfalls in Single World, but it is often entered with exaggerated fears. It is an environment in which it can be relatively easy to meet strangers and make friends, but there are risks involved. These risks, however, are much less than those in Casual World, the arena of singles bars and dating services.

The primary reason for the existence of singles clubs is to provide functions and activities so that single people can meet, date, and develop relationships with people of the opposite sex. For many members, an additional goal is remarriage. So how do you go about meeting that certain person? Attend the functions; there is no other way.

The singles clubs are excellent places to go to alleviate the loneliness that is often concomitant with being newly single, and the more functions you attend, the sooner you'll establish a meaningful support network. Then things get much better. Once you've made friends among both sexes, you'll be inclined to attend more of the functions because you'll know your friends will be there and you won't feel alone, strange, or isolated.

Another important goal of singles clubs is to help people adjust to being single. One member put it well when he said, "Living alone constructively and liking it is the prevailing emphasis of most clubs...even those sponsored by churches."

DATING AND RELATING IN SINGLE WORLD

Relationships between singles vary in length and in structure. They last anywhere from one month to several years, and some develop into remarriages, though live-in arrangements are also common. There are also couples who prefer to live separately, perhaps because of children, but limit their dating to each other. They "go steady," much like young people do.

Single World also readily accommodates those who play the field continually, with the constant influx of new faces providing a never-ending source of new dates. Remember, in singles clubs the principal shared interest of the members is to meet people of the opposite sex, and you'll be able to informally screen potential dates and relates. If you sense possible interest from someone who attracts you, you can inquire about them. You can suggest going for coffee after the meeting, and you can do this whether you're a man or a woman. After a number of raps and get-togethers, you get to know the person as an individual and can better determine if the two of you share any interests and if the person has the attributes, personality, and values you are looking for.

Dating in the singles clubs is trial and error, but at least you know a little bit about each other. Both of you are known quantities with reputations, hence less time, money, and effort is wasted dating disappointing strangers — as might result, for example, if you used a dating service. On the other hand, in Single World there is a tendency for a few people to "fall into" relationships and remain there only for the sake of convenience. When this happens, those involved temporarily impair opportunities to date others and maybe find Mr. or Ms. Reasonably Right. People are certainly reluctant to ask out a person who is currently involved.

REMARRIAGES IN SINGLE WORLD

Those who are eager to remarry find that although it is relatively easy to meet people quickly in a singles club, and even to date and become intimate, it's rather difficult to find that special someone (as it is everywhere, for that matter), like looking for the proverbial needle in a haystack. After all, Single World is composed of people with a wide assortment of values and almost every kind of background. The only thing you can be sure you have in common with other members is the desire to meet new friends, date, and possibly remate.

However, good relationships and good marriages can and do emerge from Single World. It's just that it often takes a lot of time and effort along with more than a little bit of luck to find Mr. or Ms. Reasonably Right in this milieu. Six times out of ten the strangers you meet and date so easily in a singles club will turn out to have nothing in common with you except loneliness, unhappiness, financial worries, or other problems. There are quite a few Single World participants you won't even consider dating. If you are looking for a new Mr. or Ms. Reasonably Right, expect any search in Single World to be a long one. Try to make it an enjoyable one as well. Why not decide ahead of time that it is premature to think about remating and just relax and have a good time?

Some people are unable or unwilling for job-related or personal reasons to wean themselves from Single World, and they indefinitely retain the clubs as their primary social outlets. Others want to remate but are unable to eliminate their negatives sufficiently to relate to another person long-term. Still others postpone remarriage for family reasons. For example, those still raising children often prefer to stay single because of the trauma involved in remating. Step-parenting is a difficult undertaking at best, and remarriages involving children are often imperiled by having kids at home. They threaten a remarriage more than any other factor, including sexual incompatibility and financial disagreement. Many therefore stay single until the kids leave. While a good case can be made for risking remarriage if the kids are still very young, up to age eight or so, with teenagers at home the risks increase substantially. Whether or not to remarry in such instances largely depends on the individual qualities and personalities of both the children and the adults. There are no ironclad rules.

CHOOSING SINGLES CLUBS

Depending on where you live, you will find different kinds of singles clubs to accommodate different kinds of people. The atmosphere of a club depends on who runs it and the kind of people it attracts. After you have established yourself in one club, you'll hear about others. Try a few. There is substantial cross-membership and drifting between clubs. If you're more comfortable in one than the others, that's where you'll end up spending most of your time.

If you join a club and decide it's not for you, simply stop going and stop paying dues. Then try another club. A club you were comfortable with at first may no longer meet your needs after you have become more experienced. That's okay, too. With your experience, you'll know what you want and how to accomplish it.

Dr. Theodore Machler wrote: "People often steer away from singles organizations because they feel that to join is an admission of failure or inadequacy. I don't think that is true at all, because meeting people through singles organizations makes more sense than some of our other selection processes. It's very reasonable for single people to look for single people — singles groups are a logical thing."

Be logical. Force yourself to join and become active in at least one club.

A surprising variety of nonprofit, commercial, and church-sponsored singles groups is available, but don't allow yourself to become anxious about picking the "right" one. If you are not content with the first one you pick, try another one simultaneously. In the end, you may find yourself regularly attending three clubs — even more. By this time you will have learned that you are never going to find one that is perfect for you. Like people, singles clubs simply don't come that way. Fortunately, you will also have learned how to concentrate your time and enjoy the people you really like, while remaining tolerant, considerate, and at least polite to those you don't particularly care for.

JOINING A SINGLES CLUB

Join at least one singles club as soon as you are emotionally able. This cannot be stressed too much. Then become active. Many clubs, especially the national ones, have meetings or activities scheduled seven nights a week; you'll always have something you can go to. Moreover, the process of joining a singles club is simplicity itself. Generally, all you need to do is show up and sign up.

Active members recognize that for some singles it's very difficult to begin attending meetings, rap sessions, and parties. They've been through it themselves, can sympathize, and often go out of their way to be welcoming and helpful. Think of it this way: Once you've walked through the doors you will have taken a big step toward changing your life.

Motivating yourself doesn't stop there, though. If you are like many of us, you will initially need to force yourself again and again to attend the various functions and keep going back. Stick with it and sooner than you might think the initial nervousness and self-consciousness will subside and you'll begin to feel comfortable. As you become accustomed to attending the functions, people begin to recognize you and you can put the names to the faces of one-time strangers. Your "Hi, Pat" and "Hi, Joe" will soon elicit "Hi, You" from the other members. In six months to a year, you'll not only feel like a regular member, you'll be one.

What is required is courage, persistence, and an open mind — qualities I, along with many others, found needed improvement. I now know my deficiency in these resulted in unnecessarily pro-longing my miserable period of initial loneliness, which was bad enough to make me feel alone even in a crowd. Also, my long-held opinion of singles clubs was negative, and I secretly felt that divorced people were losers. Some are, but so are some married couples, like those who will eat an entire meal in a restaurant without exchanging a single word. It's not surprising that it was several months after my divorce before I joined a singles club, and then several more months before I began to attend the functions with any regularity. I did better than some people, though. Many singles give up altogether after only a few visits.

Substantial mingling and turnover is common in all singles clubs. Those on the lookout for Mr. or Ms. Reasonably Right will move from one club to another, constantly searching. Affluent, active people sometimes belong to two or three clubs simultaneously and frequent them all for a while. They usually absent themselves during relationships but return after the breakups. Some marry and leave permanently. Others leave permanently because they find the minimal behavioral demands of Single World too burdensome and concentrate their social lives in singles bars and the transient lifestyle of Casual World. Newly single people often go so far as to join a singles club, but after attending only a function or two, quit going and never return.

I hope that you won't make this mistake, that you'll gather your courage early on and stay until you have enough experience to judge if this is for you. Something is scheduled by many singles clubs every night of the week — parties, dances, group discussions, lectures, and more. Take advantage of the dating opportunities they provide.

Another benefit of the clubs is the opportunity for personal growth. Here is what one woman wrote in a letter to the editor of a club newsletter when she decided to give up the office she held, leave the club, and settle down:

> Is there life beyond PWP (Parents Without Part-
> ners)?...Now the time has come to move into the real world
> and squarely face the challenges beyond PWP. For me, life
> beyond PWP means energetically pursuing my career objec-
> tives. It means sharing my life with someone special...I've
> enjoyed my life in PWP and appreciate the opportunity to
> learn, to grow, and to share my experiences along the way.
> The interpersonal skills and communications techniques
> I've acquired have become part of my treasure chest of
> assets and are used daily in my business and personal
> life...Was it worth it? Absolutely!

BACKGROUNDS OF MEMBERS

People come to most (but not all) of the clubs from different social, economic, and educational backgrounds. This diversity can be stimulating to some, but it often is initially troublesome to others who find so many of the members "different." When you were married did your friends come from a wide segment of society? Probably not. If you're like most of us, you stayed within your own social sphere, a homogeneous group of people. As a member of a singles club, you'll háve the opportunity to associate with a much wider cross section of people. Keep an open mind and be tolerant; it can be educational and rewarding. You can select your own circle of friends from among those you meet and like.

Most clubs include both widowed and divorced people, though their backgrounds differ in important ways. One widower wrote: "Comparing my problems as a widower to those of my divorced friends, I can only conclude that being divorced is far worse. It is the most degrading experience that is commonly available. Your closest and most intimate friend becomes your enemy, and society brands you a failure. Small wonder that so many divorced people are fearful, bitter, humiliated, and depressed."

It's true that many divorced singles are initially bitter, but a good number will recover and find mates. Others wallow in self-pity and carry on as though their lives were over — and so they are unless they change their ways.

You'll meet all kinds of people, and you'll need to be both tolerant and tactful in your dealings with some of the people at the clubs. Aside from the minority with severe psychological problems or alcohol or drug addictions, you'll bump into perfectly normal people who are temporarily behaving abnormally because of recent trauma. In this category are individuals driven by a zealous compulsion to remarry or show a former spouse that they are still desirable. Here and there you'll find singles with the need to dominate, and you'll meet a few with the need to be dominated — by anyone who can provide emotional or financial support and make their decisions for them. More often, you will be preempted by the fiercely aggressive "independent" people who stridently proclaim they have "found themselves" and found "freedom." Be prepared to meet all kinds of personalities.

PARENTS WITHOUT PARTNERS

The national nonprofit organization Parents Without Partners (PWP) probably has a chapter near you, and PWP is as good as any other singles club to use as a starting point. Membership fees are nominal, and the only requirements for membership in PWP are good character and parenthood. Your children can be newborns or married adults; they can be living with you, your ex-spouse, or on their own. As far as ascertaining good character is concerned, PWP does what it can by requiring a recommendation from a minister, doctor, lawyer, or other professional — usually easily obtainable. Although it includes programs and activities for children, PWP is, in effect, a singles club. It has most of the same activities other singles clubs offer: group discussions, house parties, happy hours, picnics, dances, dance instruction, tennis, bowling, biking, hiking, camping, and more, depending on the size of the chapter.

Of all the singles clubs, PWP is the most heterogeneous, including people of all ages and economic and educational levels. Most come from the middle class, with the center of gravity falling toward the lower rather than the higher end of the economic scale. Affluent, well-educated singles are also represented, however. The members come and go, while a nucleus group usually remains. As with any group, there are cliques. It's natural for people with similar values and interests to gather together. In time you'll possibly stake out your own circle of friends.

Much casual trial-and-error dating takes place. Relationships form easily and last anywhere from several weeks to several years. PWP pairings do result in lasting remarriages and other permanent arrangements, but not nearly as often as many would hope. That seems to happen more often outside the clubs, in Real World rather than Single World. When a remarriage does occur but fails, which is not at all uncommon, both partners frequently return to the same club and begin dating again.

PWP holds annual elections of officers, and as in most organizations, the old-timers tend to dominate the key posts. They do the planning, head the committees, do the nuts and bolts work, open up their houses for parties and discussions, and prepare and distribute the bulletins and calendars of events — making close friends in the process.

The cooperative nature of PWP is typical of the church-sponsored singles clubs as well, though church officials sometimes contribute significantly. However, the commercial clubs operate differently; everything relating to organization, functions, finances, and activities is planned and controlled by the managers and owners. These clubs are businesses and exist to make profits.

COMMERCIAL CLUBS

The commercial singles clubs in my locale, the Tampa-St. Petersburg-Clearwater area of Florida, are representative of the clubs found in most medium-to-large cities. One of these, Coast to Coast Singles, is a good example of the many self-styled middle-class clubs. "A typical member is at the top of intelligence quotients," claims the proprietor. "Many are affluent, most are successful in their jobs and careers, with a small number, usually young mothers, on rather tight budgets." No proof of affluence or intelligence was evident to me, and the social and economic status of the membership seemed similar to that of PWP.

A host of other commercial clubs exists in this area, some of them having been in business for only a short while. Because of the vulnerability of lonely single people, there is a temptation to exploit them financially. You need to be aware of this. Travel and dance promotions are especially frequent, and pressures to participate are difficult to resist. Seldom are clubs out-and-out fraudulent, but it happens. One local promoter was charged with grand theft for selling cruises that were not available.

Despite claims to the contrary, it really isn't possible to maintain uniformly "high quality" membership as long as the club is open to the general public. On the other hand, there are first-rate people in just about all the clubs. The responsibility for choosing your new single friends is yours, and yours alone.

The commercial clubs which advertise in newspapers, magazines, or on television often have a difficult time financially. Like most other clubs, these for-profit clubs offer cocktail parties, dances, rap sessions, and travel opportunities — all the usual. It's just that a few are more posh and do things up more expensively than, for example, PWP. They typically pitch costly travel opportunities and financial planning.

The now-defunct Turning Point in my area was an excellent example of this type of club. Its advertising boasted that many of the members had college degrees and otherwise implied that the club was the best place to meet upscale singles and experience exotic activities — thus justifying an unusually high membership fee. Plagued by a shortage of eligible men, like most other clubs, the Turning Point began discounting membership fees for males, just as some dance studios do. Even so, it eventually went bankrupt and abruptly closed its doors, leaving its members holding a very large but empty financial bag.

Chapter Two was yet another such club in my area. Boasting that it limited its membership to professionals, its membership was depleted by fierce competition abetted by the fickleness and faddishness of many singles, and it too faded from the scene. Clubs continually appear and disappear. Whether or not comparable clubs designed to meet the burgeoning demand of yuppies, like Tampa Executive Singles and The Party, will stay in business remains to be seen.

PRIVATE CLUBS

If you are financially well off, you can find singles clubs which attract only the richer and better educated people and are more homogeneous. Sometimes people will join affluent clubs they can ill afford, because they are looking for rich mates. Few succeed. The initiation fees, ongoing expenses, and perhaps the overall inability to "fit in" tend to discourage their continued membership .

Some degree of uniformity or "quality" exists in the unadvertised private clubs that members join by invitation only. They are run by operators skilled in sophisticated methods of screening out those they consider unsuitable or subtly discouraging their continued attendance. In some of the invitation-only clubs, snobbery exists. One member pompously declared, "We are the elite," and her tongue was not in her cheek. Don't be put off by the few snobs you may find in the more affluent clubs. Many splendid people are there, too, just as there are first-rate people in the clubs where the financial center of gravity is not so high. By contrast, the really wealthy and famous are almost never found in any kind of singles club, though once in a while you read about a millionaires club. People in the highest reaches experience little difficulty attracting dates, relates, and remates on their own.

A unique by-invitation-only club seeking to maintain a fifty-fifty ratio of men and women has lasted for almost a decade here — difficult to accomplish in the middle age set. The club, promoted mainly by word of mouth, is run by a woman who also operates a travel agency. Candidates are informally screened for compatibility, although standards are seemingly applied more rigidly to female candidates than to males. This organization, the Adventure Travel Club, omits rap sessions and concentrates on parties, dances, and, in particular, travel. Cruises, resort vacations, out-of-town theater trips, and golf and tennis weekends are all arranged and promoted by the director. Her social connections, skill, and personality are the primary reasons the club has exhibited remarkable staying power.

It might surprise most readers that many members of the Adventure Travel Club, myself included, also belong to PWP. A lot of crossover between clubs exists, and if you happen to have the time or money for just one club, then PWP would be a good choice — unless you have a strong religious orientation.

CHURCH-SPONSORED SINGLES CLUBS

The different kinds of people, the different values, and the different lifestyles in clubs like PWP and its commercial counterparts may sometimes seem like just too much. But don't give up. If you know absolutely that the secular clubs are not for you, then join a church-sponsored singles club.

Religious organizations have recently begun to sponsor singles groups at a rate approaching the demand. As a result, religious organizations are once again becoming important meeting grounds for the sexes, like they were many years ago. While remarriage is considered the most desirable outcome for couples who meet in church-sponsored clubs, the clubs increasingly recognize that many of the divorced are not ready for remarriage — that their members need to work through their emotional problems before they can successfully relate to other people on a permanent basis.

To generalize about the singles groups within different denominations — or even within the same denomination but in different churches — is difficult. It is safe to say, though, that all the church groups seek to provide their members with wholesome and moral social lives within a spiritual framework. Even though leadership of the church clubs is always dominated by members of the sponsoring denomination, membership is often open to all comers. Membership fees usually are either nominal or nonexistent.

The activities of the church-sponsored clubs are similar to those in the secular clubs. The overall tone of the church groups is more conservative, however, though even this is not uniformly true (Unitarian groups, for example, tend to be quite liberal). The rap sessions in church-sponsored clubs are less likely to deal with sex, and sexual overtones and initiatives tend to be muted. The same conservatism applies to drinking and drug taking; both are much less in evidence than in secular clubs. Another important difference is that the church clubs often provide baby-sitting services during their activities, a practice seldom found in the secular clubs and a big plus for the "eight is enough" set.

One representative church-sponsored singles club in my area is Faith United Singles, which meets weekly at a Presbyterian church recreation hall. Brief opening remarks are made by a young minister; forthcoming events are announced by the club's officers; and then the members segregate into small groups for discussions. Following the rap sessions is a social hour with coffee and dessert. The Faith United club, like many church-sponsored groups, also emphasizes activities in which children can participate with their parents. Camping, volleyball, skating, and sight-seeing are a few of them. In the adults-only meetings and parties, alcohol is not served, but some members meet for drinks and dancing afterwards in a nearby cocktail lounge. Most members, however, gather at an inexpensive restaurant for conversation, laughter, coffee, and dessert.

Other Protestant denominations have conservative but active singles ministries. The Baptist group, for example, emphasizes Bible study but also offers a full range of activities for singles and has a large local following.

On the more liberal end of the local spectrum is the club sponsored by the Unitarian-Universalists. The group offers most of the same activities as Faith United, but the atmosphere is different. For one thing, social drinking, though not allowed on church premises, is allowed at the parties. There are the usual picnics, dances, and discussions, and in addition a regular Sunday brunch following church services.

The Jewish singles clubs in my area are loosely affiliated with the Jewish Community Center, and an effort is made to encourage spiritual growth and Jewish cohesiveness. Membership includes single adults of all ages, and the usual activities are offered. Sometimes the group visits area lounges and restaurants for a happy hour and dinner. Local Catholic churches also sponsor singles organizations, which are usually referred to as support groups for the widowed and divorced.

THE STAR OF THE SHOW

Shakespeare pointed out that all the world is a stage and that we are merely the players. So far in this chapter we've described the shape and dimensions of the Single World stage and the various sets that are available. Before proceeding you need to know more about the players upon whom the success or failure of your play will depend.

No matter how anxious, how depressed, how guilty, or how inadequate you feel, sooner or later you're going to realize that you're the star, and that sooner or later you'll have to come out front-stage-center in full view of the stage lights illuminating Single World. No longer can you tolerate hiding in the gloomy shadows of your darkened living room illuminated only by your television set. Unless you've begun to build a satisfying social life elsewhere, preferably in Real World, then staying at home will eventually become intolerable and you'll be forced to attempt the Single World stage. Fortunately, the play does not call for you to appear on stage in any significant way during the early scenes, so you've got a little time to pause and think.

To begin with, you know that only rarely is anyone comfortable about appearing in a new play, so it will be natural for you to feel nervous. Try not to show it, however. Some famous actors admit to throwing up before going on stage, only to appear perfectly calm, collected, and assured in their roles. Beyond that, realize that you don't need to say or do much in your early performances. You're there to try to get the feel of the club and maybe to make a few friendly acquaintances. Just this much can be a big victory over a single person's nervous inhibitions.

You may leave some or even most of your early club functions feeling alone and empty, wondering if it's all worth the trouble. That's normal. Keep going, it gets better. Each time you go, be willing to seek out friendly acquaintances and try to build tentative friendships. Be kind and friendly to everyone; practice the golden rule. Locate and cultivate a few same-sex acquaintances you admire and try to become their friends, hoping they will share their experience with you. They are in a position to help you adjust.

Put a premium on character rather than on good looks when evaluating members of both sexes as potential friends. If you're like me, you're no matinee idol yourself, though we both might have a lot to offer the right person. All too often the very handsome or strikingly beautiful are badly flawed, spoiled, or neurotic (as are many not so well endowed). Simply follow the old admonition to first look for character.

Also look inward objectively. Never underestimate your own worth. When you are feeling down and depressed, it might seem to you that you have little to offer. Why should that spouse have wanted a divorce, otherwise? (Could it have been because of his or her own shortcomings?) One of the most difficult appraisals to come by is a fair estimate of oneself, and the tendency for newly divorced people in particular is to greatly underestimate (or overestimate) themselves. Be aware of this. Give yourself a "C" at first and consider yourself an "average" member of the group. You can better estimate where you stand by observing how others react to you over a period of time.

THE SUPPORTING CAST

In assessing the people you will meet in Single World, as well as in Real World, beware of the one-glance-and-you're-out syndrome. There is a tendency of many people to sweep the room with one quick glance, and based on the meager input of superficial attractiveness, to instantly relegate the majority as not worth bothering about. A fortunate few remain the targets for the night.

This kind of self-defeating behavior originates in part from years of watching the glamorous, plastic people who star on television and screen. How many people do you know who always wear the latest fashions, whose makeup is always perfect, who never need a shave, or whose muscles bulge with power? For the most part those beautiful people are not at all representative of the real people who populate Real World — or populate Single World.

Ken Howard, star of "The White Shadow" TV series a few years ago, appeared on "The Dick Cavett Show" and came across as the nice, intelligent, pleasant, warm, and successful man he undoubtedly is. Most discriminating and intelligent women who were unaware of his celebrity would be attracted to him if they had the opportunity to talk to him and get to know him. However, the couch potatoes who limit their "possibles" to only virile, handsome men might simply write him off as "nothing special." In real life, minus toupee, makeup, and the Hollywood glamor touch, Howard indeed looks like an ordinary mortal who lives down the street and maybe owns the hardware store.

By all means don't adopt the one-glance-and-you're-out syndrome. Keep an open mind and get to know people as individuals. If by a great stroke of luck you do bump into a charming person who looks like a matinee idol or a sex goddess, look deeper. He or she might be God's gift to mankind, or merely an egotistical, selfish bore. Often if people look too good to be true, they are.

While married individuals have abundant time to devote to jobs, church, relatives, friends, hobbies, and other interests, singles often spend most of their free time searching for the opposite sex. Some are preoccupied in a search for Mr. or Ms. Wonderful, while others are looking for a succession of temporary partners with whom to enjoy "good times." You'll find that newcomers who are furtively, single-mindedly seeking instant marriage partners are actually poor prospects. They are simply not ready. At the other end of the spectrum you'll meet veteran singles with five to ten years' experience chasing partners and seeking sexual encounters of the frequent kind. Avoid them; they may never be ready.

Also steer clear of the drug and alcohol troubled individuals who need to eliminate these negatives before they can relate well. Tactfully and politely give wide berth to severely troubled men and women, too. Many have had unhappy childhoods or devastating marital experiences that have resulted in their becoming bitter and distrustful. They "know" no relationship they enter can last, and they're right; their own anger and distrust will tear it apart. Some eventually do come to realize that they are the source of their problems, but as a newcomer with problems of your own, you would do well to avoid them.

Fortunately, there is a lot of wheat among the chaff. Liberally mixed in with the stunted are the growing. Maybe somewhat shy and still unsure of themselves, they are making a successful effort to begin changing their lives to positive channels. Make an effort to make friends of both sexes in this category. Attend the functions, not just once or twice a week, but even three or four times if your schedule permits.

EXPERIENCE: THE GREAT TEACHER

Experience will teach you patience and reward you if you tackle Single World and persist. Experience will teach you something else if you got a divorce in part because you believed the popular myth portraying the singles scene as fun and games populated by laughing, self-assured, affluent, sexy, and attractive players cavorting in one glamorous setting after another.

As a single person, you do have a chance to build a satisfying life for yourself — maybe not in quite the same way as married people, but a good life nevertheless. What you make of it is up to you. You'll increase the odds to be among life's winners if you simultaneously become active in Real World and Single World, and if you regularly and dependably attend the activities of the groups you belong to — and if you never, ever dismiss someone on the basis of a single glance.

Now you are familiar with the stage, the sets, the star of the show, and the supporting cast. Let the play begin! How do you join a club? What can you expect at those scary first meetings? How do you conduct yourself? How do you get dates? You begin by beginning, and the next chapter tells you how — step by step.

6.
Falling in Love with Love

As you get ready to take the plunge and join your first singles club, the one thing that can help you the most is the company and support of a single friend or friendly acquaintance. If that friend is already a member of a singles club, you're a big step ahead of the crowd. Meeting new people and being accepted by them is always much easier when a mutual friend introduces you. Even another newly single person who signs up with you and accompanies you to the first several meetings will greatly ease the stress on your nervous system. So think hard and write down the names of same-sex single people you know and believe you could relate to fairly well. Then, if you know anyone, force yourself to pick up the phone and recruit him or her to go with you; if not, you'll have to do it the way most newly single people do — by forcing themselves to go and make friends on their own.

CHOOSING YOUR FIRST CLUB

Which club? A good place to start is Parents Without Partners, or if you think you'd be more comfortable in a religious group, ask your minister, rabbi, or priest for a recommendation. Actually, your first choice is not that crucial, and like many other singles, you might wind up belonging to two or three clubs. The important thing is to take that difficult first step. In time you'll learn from the friends you make about the other clubs in the community and you'll gravitate over the next year or two to those you prefer.

What are the actual steps you take to join? Let's use the "worst" case as an example. You are acting alone, without the benefit of another single, because you simply don't know anybody to go along with you. Pick up your telephone book and look in the white pages for Parents Without Partners (PWP). This nonprofit, inexpensive organization has all the characteristics and functions of a singles club and can usually be found even in small communities. The club is for people of all ages, and it is not necessary that your children live with you.

If you're not a parent, you might look in the Yellow Pages for commercial singles clubs. Bear in mind, however, that some are fly-by-night and exploitive, that they almost always cost substantially more than PWP, and that they don't necessarily offer as much. So tread warily. For some of you, a better idea is to join a church-sponsored club, even if you're not particularly religious. You'll learn the reputations of some of the secular clubs from members who belong to both, or have had bad experiences with one or another.

I personally started with PWP because an acquaintance told me about it. Once there, I started hearing about the other singles clubs. It took about a year before I became really familiar with what was going on in the local singles scene. There is easy access to an informal network that keeps involved singles abreast of the emergence and disappearance — and the quality — of all the various singles clubs in town.

GETTING UP YOUR NERVE

Before you pick up the phone to get instructions for joining your first club, promise yourself that you will not only go to one meeting but will follow up and go to several more. Realize that you will be nervous, but tell yourself that you will not allow this initial nervousness to stop you from living your life. You're the one in control, not your groundless fears of the unknown. Expect to be tense; everyone is the first time.

Anticipate that your first impulse may very well be to run. Your second impulse, so you'll have an excuse to run, will be to judge the people harshly. The single lifestyle you see will be quite different from what you were accustomed to as a married person, and the impulse to flee might be further fueled by using the excuse that the people you see aren't up to your standards. Many may not be, but some will be much higher up on life's totem pole than you or I will ever be. You'll never have the opportunity to pick and choose the good ones unless you attend the meetings.

It takes about six months of regular attendance to begin to know the members, gain a measure of acceptance, and begin to enjoy yourself. Unfortunately, many people join, pay their dues, and then disappear after attending only one or two functions. Cross your heart and swear that you're not going to pay your initiation fees and dues only to chicken out and lose out on all those parties, raps, dates, and friends.

Having thus resolved to join and give a club a fair trial, go ahead and pick up the telephone and dial the number of PWP or whatever alternative you have chosen. Usually a friendly voice will answer your call. Say you're interested in joining, and the woman (usually) on the other end of the line will take it from there. She won't go into a lot of detail; mostly she'll just tell you where and when the next orientation meeting for newcomers is to be held. It's there that you'll be given full details about the club and how to join.

YOUR FIRST MEETING

You've taken the plunge and called. That part, at least, wasn't too hard. Now you're on your way to the orientation meeting, and you're nervous. Maybe it's been a long time since you've gone to any social function by yourself. More than once you have to fight off an impulse to turn around and go home. You force yourself to drive on, and you arrive just about on time. The meeting places vary — sometimes in office buildings, sometimes in church recreation halls, often in members' homes. Let's say your orientation is in a home, and there are about twenty to thirty people crowded into a small living room. You sit down on a kitchen chair squeezed into a corner, and not exactly relaxed, you wait while a little more time is allowed for latecomers to arrive.

You notice that the people around you are informally and inexpensively but, for the most part, neatly dressed. There are a few with well-worn clothing indicating they might be in difficult financial circumstances. The room is fairly quiet, with only a few people managing to exchange some small talk. With relief, you notice that at least you're not nearly as nervous as you were driving over. A few late arrivals come through the door. Glancing at them and the others, you see a few people you think you might be able to relate to. A much larger number you relegate to limbo. Then you remember that you're not going to fall victim to the one-glance-and-you're-out syndrome, and you resolve to keep an open mind.

The person in charge, an experienced man or woman or a team consisting of both, welcomes this week's quota of potential recruits. You begin to realize that there is a multitude of divorced and widowed people and that you're not unique in this regard. If you must be miserable for a while, at least you'll have company. Moreover, the veteran members of the orientation team are talking and laughing. They don't look at all miserable.

After opening comments, the leader describes PWP to the

newcomers. Included is a brief history and outline of the purposes of the nonprofit organization. The various kinds of social functions are described, and everyone is given a copy of the most recent issue of the monthly bulletin or newsletter, which contains a calendar of events scheduled for the next month.

Be sure to look the calendar over when you get home; it will become very important to you. A quick glance will tell you that at least one party or dance is held every weekend and that committee meetings or discussions (raps) are held just about every other night of the week. If this is one of the larger chapters, you'll find most if not all of the following activities over the course of a year: picnics, TGIF's, dance lessons, tennis competitions, bicycle outings, card games, bowling, museum tours, fishing clinics, potlucks, and bridge lessons. Much more is scheduled than any person could conceivably have time for, so you'll be able to make choices. If you have children or grandchildren at home, you'll notice that the monthly schedule also lists the upcoming activities for children and their parents.

The orientation team will point out that all the activities are the responsibility of various committees, and that it takes a bit of work to put a good program together. That's why, right from the start, new members are encouraged to join one of the committees. If you have some free time, don't dismiss the idea out of hand. All that's asked is that you go to the committee meetings and offer your support in whatever way you can. Some members are idea people and good at getting things organized; others prefer to do some of the legwork — buying the food, for example, or gathering baseball bats and gloves. Whatever you do to contribute, you'll find that by getting involved and spending time in cooperation with others, you'll not only have fun, you'll make friends that will lead to dating.

Toward the close of the orientation meeting, membership applications are distributed and everyone is invited to fill out the forms and pay the modest initiation fee. You're not obligated to do this, however. Think it over, if you like. The advantage to signing up and paying your initiation fee at this meeting is that you will be more apt to return. If you join, you will be assigned an "Amigo," a veteran member who will help you get acquainted and formally introduce you at the next general meeting.

After the completed applications and fees are collected, coffee and dessert are offered — as at most meetings. After you've been in the club a while, you'll want to circulate, meet people, and enjoy a social hour talking with friends and acquaintances. This time, if your experience is like mine, you'll feel emotionally drained after taking this big step and will want to join the majority who leave early.

Back home, the emotional safety and physical security of your own four walls — which only a few hours before seemed to be closing in on you — bring welcome relief. Thinking back, you can't remember much about what was said or about the people who were there. You know you were nervous part of the time, but it wasn't as bad as you had feared. You pick up the club's newsletter and look it over. There are a lot of activities that could replace the lonely and miserable evenings you've been spending at home. Maybe you'll try something after you've had a few days to catch your emotional breath. But for now, especially if you went to that meeting all by yourself, you deserve a pat on the back. You have scored a small victory over your fears, and that represents a good omen of things to come.

You may harbor some misgivings about future meetings. Maybe most of the crowd was too old for you, or too young, or too poor, or too affluent, or too happy, or too depressed. But if you can keep your courage up and your head high and keep going, you'll see people differently. Some will become new friends, and others friendly acquaintances. As you begin to feel comfortable with them, you'll acquire a feeling of belonging. Even if you don't begin to feel comfortable in that group, you'll learn about other clubs you can try.

If you know what to expect — and by now you do — you'll find that joining a singles club is really not that hard on your nervous system. Moreover, if you can find another newly single person to drive to the orientation with, it will be all that much easier. If you have a friend who is an experienced member of the club, it will be a breeze.

Even so, when you start attending your early functions, you'll naturally feel some tension. Expect it and accept it as part of the dues you must pay, but be assured that the tension will soon diminish. Help yourself relax by realizing that during these early meetings you don't have to say much or do anything striking or dramatic. Your acceptance by the group is best achieved slowly, over time. Get to know people, and let them get to know you. You'll make friends, and as you do, you'll have more fun and your opportunities to date will surface and start staring you in the face — literally.

RAP SESSIONS

Because the calendar of events contains so many offerings, choose according to your preferences. By all means, though, include a number of rap sessions. These informal discussion meetings are usually well attended and represent opportunities to meet many of the members. Most newcomers enjoy the raps because they're informal, lighthearted, humorous, and just plain fun. No experienced single will take what is said too seriously.

Early on, self-consciousness hindered my efforts to enjoy the dances and parties, but I found I could attend a rap session and feel somewhat comfortable even though I said little or nothing. Later on, the rap session continued to constitute the environment I preferred for getting to know people — even as an experienced single.

At a typical rap the participants gather in a living room, much as earlier described. An experienced moderator opens the discussion when the members have all arrived, often shortly after 8:00 p.m. He introduces the topic, which was announced in the bulletin, and provides some background information, perhaps quoting a few experts or tossing out a few thoughts of his own. Then the floor is opened to discussion.

There are times when you should take what is said with a grain of salt. Accomplishments, especially in the sexual realm, go beyond belief. Much of it is tongue-in-cheek humor. Generally people tend to say what they think will please or entertain the others, not what they think will inform them.

Don't feel compelled to talk during the first few raps. You're certainly welcome to join in, but feel free to just look around, listen, and get a feel for the singles scene. Study some of the people and listen with the idea of learning what they're like. As you become more comfortable with the group, you'll naturally and unself-consciously begin to participate in the discussions. Don't worry too much about what you say. The idea is just to let the others know a little bit about you.

Discussion topics at the rap sessions will be quite different from those you have been familiar with at the social gatherings of your married friends — unless your old pals liked to talk about sex a lot. Little is said about babies or recipes, and what you hear openly discussed in mixed singles circles may surprise you. If such frank, open talk makes you uncomfortable, consider sampling the rap sessions at a church-sponsored singles group.

Singles clubs schedule discussion topics of particular interest to singles and of value in helping them deal with emotional problems. Here is a sampling of topics from a recent PWP schedule:

> Becoming a Winner with Yourself
> How to Select Your Mate
> Why Me?
> Loneliness
> The Four Stages of a Date
> Setting New Directions
> The Four Demons: Fear, Hostility, Inferiority, Guilt
> How to Combat Holiday Blues
> Who Am I Really Looking For?
> Is Beauty Only Skin Deep?
> Are You Afraid to Get Involved?

At any rap you attend, always bear in mind that the principal motives that bring people to these meetings are to escape loneliness and find companionship and/or a sex partner and perhaps to find Mr. or Ms. Reasonably Right. Of course, many have a secondary interest in learning about the topic of discussion, but for the most part, people go to raps to socialize.

One of the things that may surprise you if you are well into middle age is the fact that not only the young people, but your peers as well, participate in discussing the full range of birds-and-bees topics. Of course, those not interested don't come; those who do come want to meet others who are interested. The participants are far too intelligent and sophisticated to use such juvenile designations as "dirty old man" and "dirty old lady." It's strange that it still takes courage to say that sex is not only clean, natural, and healthy, but also thoroughly enjoyable for mature adults. So if you're in mature middle age and looking for an intimate relationship or a remating, don't be reluctant about going to a rap billed "Should They or Shouldn't They?"

Whatever the rap topic, try to arrive only ten to fifteen minutes before the scheduled time. If you arrive earlier, you may inconvenience your host, who may still be busy cleaning up after dinner, making baby-sitting arrangements, taking a shower, or whatever. Try not to be among the last arrivals, however, because the crowd often exceeds the living room seating capacity and latecomers often have the pleasure of sitting on the floor.

If you're shy, you'll probably sit in the closest empty chair without looking to see who else is in the room. That's okay, but it does cheat you out of a chance to sit beside someone you might have seen at your orientation and tentatively liked or beside someone else who attracts you. Feel free to use the time before the rap begins to get acquainted. Don't be bashful about consciously seeking out other people you might want to get to know during the social hour after the rap. Remember, everyone there wants to enlarge his or her circle of friends. Be sure to speak loud enough for those interested in you to hear your name when introductions are made at the beginning of the rap. Often the members are asked to give their names and maybe tell how long they've been single or been members of the club. Don't be so self-conscious waiting your turn that you miss the names of the people who attract you.

During the rap, don't allow yourself to become upset or alienated by the behavior of a few you don't like. Simply pass up, tactfully and politely, the people and ideas you're not enamored of. Never get angry or argue. Instead, wait patiently for the discussion hour to end and the social hour to begin. After you've become experienced, you'll realize that the period after the rap is when you make your introductions, get telephone numbers, and maybe arrange for after-rap coffee or a drink with someone who attracts you, or with a small group of friends.

BREAKING THE ICE

If your experience is similar to what I went through during the first few raps, you'll have to fight off the impulse to leave and go home as soon as the discussion begins. Stick around at least long enough to make one or two friendly acquaintances you'll recognize and talk to the next time. Don't join the people who leave early, even though you may feel a strong urge to do so.

Instead, follow the crowd as it moves over to the dining room table for cookies and coffee, take some yourself, and head back to the living room, where you'll see people standing and socializing. Keep reminding yourself over and over that all the people are there to meet other people, especially the opposite sex — just like you are. It's perfectly all right to walk up to someone of either sex and introduce yourself. Go ahead, walk up to someone, give them your name, and say something — anything. The weather is nice. The rap was good. The moderator was interesting. I liked what you had to say.

What you say doesn't have to be witty or profound. Your smile is much more important. Everybody knows that the first few sentences don't really mean a thing. When people walk up to you and introduce themselves, how important is it to you what they have to say at first? It's the gesture that counts.

People in sales have little difficulty in starting conversations, but for many of the rest of us, it can be nigh impossible. Nothing says you have to initiate conversations and get to know people tonight, but you'll feel good about yourself if you do so. Nor will the process always be so nerve-wracking. Skill in breaking the ice, like anything else, comes with practice and experience. If your icebreaking leads to a series of dates, or even to Mr. or Ms. Reasonably Right, you'll surely be glad you made the effort.

Expect to occasionally encounter some awkwardness, and bear in mind that the other people may be just as nervous as you are, especially if they are newcomers too. In a combined effort to get a conversation going, neither of you has a script to provide the smooth, witty lines used by television and movie actors. The awkwardness will soon pass, and it will be easier to talk to that person in the future. Remember, finally, that if you don't take the initiative, you'll lose many opportunities to get to know people who interest you.

There are times when a small group will spontaneously decide to go out after a rap session for a drink or more coffee. It's obviously a good way to get to know people better and to let other people get to know you, so say yes if someone suggests this.

If very little happens at your first rap session or so despite your efforts, or if there seems to be no one there who interests you, be patient and go back anyway. People who share your interests and values will surface. In turn, they may introduce you to little-known singles groups where you'll find a niche that appeals to you. However, keep an open mind and be aware that people with whom you seem to have little in common can be first-rate individuals, and deserve to be treated accordingly.

SINGLES PARTIES

The acquaintances you make at the raps will help you feel more at home when you begin going to the parties. There the crowds will probably be much larger, and you'll see some people you've never met before, as some members attend only the dances and parties and seldom show up at the raps.

I had mixed feelings when I went to my first party and encountered a lot of people talking animatedly to each other. I felt miserable and out of place, and I was envious of the new arrivals who walked in and immediately spotted people they knew and went over to greet them. It seemed to me that everyone else in the room was happy, well adjusted, and had lots of friends. Only I alone, in the whole world, was miserable, lonely, and anxious.

I remember once telling someone that among the advantages of being married was the fact that you didn't have to go to a lot of dances or parties. This night I resented having to go out in the middle stage of my life to search for women to date with only the vaguest ideas about how people courted these days. Would I ever find someone? Considering the alternative — another lonely, miserable night at home with the TV — I had to force myself to go out.

It was with a degree of difficulty that I had finally found the house, which was located in an older middle-class neighborhood. I knew I had arrived at the right place when I saw a large number of cars parked up and down both sides of the street. I parked and smoked a last cigarette, then I resolutely marched up to the house. I was somewhat annoyed by the blaring disco music, and I wondered why these forty- and fifty-year-olds weren't listening to romantic ballads or show tunes. That's how out of touch I was.

I was worried that I wouldn't know anybody there since I had only recently joined PWP. I did know the hostess, however, from one of the rap sessions. She was a tall and slim, pleasant and energetic woman of about forty-five who was generous in making her home available and considerate to newcomers. The fact that I knew she would be there had buttressed my courage and motivated me to go to this first party.

There was standing room only, not only in the living room, but in all the rooms. The well-worn furniture, pushed back against the walls, was fully occupied. Everywhere people were standing elbow-to-elbow, talking, laughing, drinking, and seemingly knowing everybody else and having a wonderful time — everyone but me! Terribly uncomfortable, I could see only the bad side of things — such as the boisterous few who had had too much to drink and the deafening music, which forced people practically to shout at each other.

The dining room table was covered with inexpensive potluck dishes brought by some of the members. Those of us who had come empty-handed had been required at the door to pay the usual party fee to cover the cost of potato chips, cheese and crackers, peanuts, and the like. The bar was filled with BYOB bottles, and the soft drinks and mixes were provided by the club.

I spotted a few acquaintances, people I had seen at the rap sessions, and obtained temporary relief from my feelings of awkwardness and self-consciousness by forcing myself to go over and briefly talk to them. I don't remember what I said or what they said. I felt very uncomfortable, so at the first good opportunity, I squeezed my way out of the house — quite unnoticed, I'm sure — and drove home with great relief. So much for my first singles club party.

I felt I had earned an "A" for effort, however, because I disliked parties and had forced myself to go. I subsequently attended more PWP parties, but I usually found them too loud and lively for my taste. Much later, when I had gained experience and enlarged my circle of friends, I began to go fairly regularly to other, quieter parties attended by somewhat older people. Actually, I realized all along that I was not the partying type, that I preferred intimate dinner parties and small social groups with quiet background music and stimulating discussions. However, I continued to attend a number of parties either to meet new women to date or, if I was going with someone at the time, to please her.

OTHER CLUBS, OTHER PARTIES

As my circle of single friends and acquaintances widened — and as I progressed with my research for this book — I went to parties sponsored by many different groups. Some people from PWP broke off and started a new club with the goal of attracting a more affluent membership. They referred to themselves as a club for business and professional single people, the only restriction relating to age: women from thirty to fifty and men from thirty-five to sixty. I attended a St. Patrick's Day party they held a few years after experiencing the debacle of my first singles party, and I had a really good time.

The setting was at one of the members' homes in upper middle-class suburbia. I had been invited by a friend — urged to do so, in fact — because they were going to be short of men, a chronic problem of most singles clubs here. This was my first party with the group, and I was made to feel most welcome by a pair of greeters at the door. They collected my party fee and gave me a brochure and a membership application to take home with me.

I entered the living room, which was crowded with people drinking, talking, and laughing against a background of lively but not overly loud music. The party was in full swing. Delicious hors d'oeuvres were attractively arranged and strategically placed to be convenient to everyone, including those who had spilled out onto the terrace surrounding a small swimming pool.

Though it was my first visit to a function of this club, I didn't feel at all out of place. I knew about a third of the people there, having met them at PWP or one of the other three clubs I frequented at the time. Not only did I have friends and acquaintances to talk to, but I was sufficiently experienced by then to know what to do and what to say.

What's nice about going to a function where you know lots of people is that through them you can meet still more people, and it snowballs. My friends introduced me to some of their friends, and if I'd been keeping track, I could have added at least ten names to a list of interesting new acquaintances. I eased my way in and out of conversations, and I made a point of introducing myself to a few strangers I found attractive or interesting. I also made a point of talking to some of the apparent novices who looked lost and a little forlorn. I tried to make them more comfortable and introduced them to at least one other person before moving on.

Following the cocktail hour, we enjoyed a nice buffet, neither elaborate nor expensive, but good. Because it was St. Patrick's Day, the main dish was Irish stew, served with a variety of salads and delicious desserts that had been brought in by the women. The men's responsibility had been to stock the bar.

We sat down to eat at the dining room table, or at card tables set up in the living room, the den, and on the terrace. Others sat on the couch and used the coffee table, stood at the mantle, and even sat cross-legged on the floor. The music was turned down a little while we ate.

After dinner we were treated to a pleasant hour of entertainment, which would be followed by dancing. One of the members played guitar and sang Irish ballads with a genuine brogue. After a while, he encouraged the group to join in, and we all sang "Sweet Rosie O'Grady." We sang a few more songs, getting better each time — or so we thought.

Our singing tapered off and the room was cleared for dancing. Disco, rock, jazz, and a few old romantic ballads were all played on the stereo. After some dancing, I chatted with people for a while and obtained the phone numbers of a few women. As usual, I left relatively early — partying into the wee hours had never been my cup of tea — but this time I was in a good frame of mind; I had had a good time.

Looking back, that party was not all that different from the first one, though it may have been a little more upscale. The big difference between the two had been in my attitude and mental set. A couple of years had now passed since my divorce and I had paid my dues.

FANCY SINGLES SOCIALS

Throughout my Single World explorations, I became familiar with only two local clubs that sponsored truly elaborate socials — dinners, dances, and parties. One of these was the Adventure Travel Club, described in the last chapter; the other was New Beginnings Singles. Many members of these clubs were quite well-off, but I was not surprised that some of them also belonged to PWP. Here is how the Adventure Travel Club billed an upcoming event in its newsletter:

May 12: Saturday Night Mexican Fiesta

Our fun-loving Senorita is opening her lovely water-front home for this very special occasion. This will be a catered party, but in addition there will be something very special from the grill. She will be adding to the menu with some of her own special concoctions. Wear something from "South of the Border," and bring a wide brim hat if you have one for the Mexican hat dance. There'll be music for dancing, prizes, delicious food, and fun for all!

The party was indeed fun. Another time, my art training and status as a docent at the Salvador Dali Museum were availed when I conducted a special tour for the club, followed by cocktails and dinner at a member's house.

Affluence provided the means, and the club leadership, the good taste, that made all the Adventure Travel Club events most enjoyable. However, there was one occasion, an engagement party for two of the group's couples, when they really outdid themselves. The setting was a member's high-rise condominium overlooking the Gulf of Mexico, and it was perfect, like a movie set. While we stood in small clusters enjoying conversation and cocktails in the large living room, the sun, sky, and clouds combined to present us with a spectacular red and orange sunset — the kind travel magazines love to splash on their front covers.

The hostess showed a group of us through the two-story spacious apartment. The master bedroom on the upper level, reached by a spiral staircase, overlooked an enormous living area, which had twenty-foot windows offering us our magnificent view. Richly decorated and expensively furnished, the whole of it could have easily been lifted from the pages of *House Beautiful*. As I looked around me, it crossed my mind that here was a group of singles who had a lot to be grateful for. (It also crossed my mind that the off-white carpeting might not be very practical.)

Unlike most parties, no one had been at the door to collect party fees. The party was by invitation only, and the guests had mailed their checks in. Nor was this a BYOB party; the elegant mirrored bar was well stocked. The hors d'oeuvres, artfully laid out on silver trays in the dining room, included jumbo shrimp, taco shells and guacamole dip, meat-and-pastry cakes, and miniature quiche treats. Extremely popular was a bowl of fresh cut vegetables, chilled and presented as finger food for the weight conscious, which included almost everyone present.

There was no blaring disco music here, but rather a soft, easy-listening background music providing just the right atmosphere for the buzzing conversation. The guests enjoyed a drink or two and then applauded the engaged couples.

After the social hour, the entire party moved downstairs to the clubhouse, adjacent to the pool and only yards from the ocean. About twelve tables for four had been set. There were place cards and gaily colored paper tablecloths, and the ceilings and walls were decorated with brightly colored balloons and streamers. A bouquet of fresh cut flowers and bottle of fine wine greeted the guests at each of the tables, and the roast beef dinner, like everything else, was top-of-the-line.

After dinner, the engaged couples were toasted and roasted by an articulate lawyer acting as the master of ceremonies. (The extent to which singles applaud and envy those in their midst who remarry never ceases to amaze me.) Then there was dancing, which I assume continued into the wee hours. However, after thanking the hostess and again congratulating the engaged couples, I left with the first group to exit.

Other clubs are characterized by first-rate get-togethers and first-rate people. Again, one needs to be tapped into the singles scene to gain access to them or even hear about their existence. Like most clubs except PWP, which goes on and on, these upscale clubs tend to appear and disappear over the years.

One relatively new club here, New Beginnings, not only sponsors upscale raps, dances, and the other typical singles functions, it also taps its members every now and then to put on a talent show. One show featured a humorous mock wedding, a western singer, a comedic trio pantomiming a song making fun of the Fuehrer's face, a poet reading some of her works, and a woman who, with piano accompaniment, beautifully sang some popular old show tunes. All in all, the talent show more closely resembled a "professional hour" than an "amateur hour." Incidentally, the entertainment was preceded by an opportunity for the members to socialize over wine and a delicious buffet.

SINGLES CLUB DANCES

In contrast to most Real World dances where you often come with a partner, at most Single World dances, as you might expect, coming with a date is strongly discouraged. PWP rules, which unfortunately are widely ignored, state that if you do come to a dance with someone, the date ends at the door. This rule was put into effect to encourage men to dance with more than one woman.

Both PWP newcomers and some old-timers occasionally complain that the dancing doesn't get underway soon enough. I have seen women turn down invitations to dance, but only very rarely. More frequently, I've seen women sit most of the night waiting to be asked. (I've also heard many women complain about this.) Men would do well to ask quite a few different women to dance. Not only would they meet more women that way, but it wouldn't hurt their reputations to be thought of as considerate gentlemen. Women, in turn, would be wise not to turn down any offer to dance unless, of course, the man's behavior is blatantly rude. Most singles dances have frequent ladies' choices, and it is also not considered poor form for a woman to ask a man to dance. So, ladies, if the circumstances are appropriate, feel free to gather your courage and ask that interesting man for the next rumba. Few men are ignorant or callous enough to turn you down.

A well-informed woman who looked over this chapter for me wrote in the margin:

> I have never understood people who attend dances but have no intention of dancing. It obviously is a poor place to engage in meaningful conversation. Please don't reject a dance with a person. It took them a lot of courage to ask. Most of us have fragile egos and feel insecure enough at

these functions. If you do ask, and you are rejected, a friend of mine gave me some expressions that always leave you with the last word (and show you have a sense of humor). If you are a guy and have just been told no, say, "I guess this means marriage is out." If you are a woman, say, "I guess this means sex is out." Be sure to say it with a smile and then turn on your heel. They lost their chance!

Whether you choose to use some kind of remark like this or no — and I personally wouldn't bother if it happened to me — don't let the possibility of rejection keep you from asking for a dance.

Nor should you let the fact that your dancing might be rusty or still awkward inhibit you. These days very wide latitude is allowed for what passes for dancing. Look at most of the couples on the floor and you'll agree. Sure, a few couples look like they were born wearing dancing shoes, but most of the rest are like you and me.

For men, who will subsequently have to call to ask for dates, this is a good opportunity to start looking. If you receive any kind of encouraging signals from the woman you're dancing with, then muster your courage and ask her if you might call sometime. On the other hand, you'll know an unpromising situation by the studied boredom, silence, and obvious disinterest. Then don't bother. While you shouldn't let the fact that you're not a particularly good dancer hold you back, and even though you'll see plenty of other mediocre dancers on the floor, if you like to dance, improve your ability by taking a few lessons. Sometimes singles clubs offer inexpensive lessons; and you're right, it's another place to meet people. Some singles even become expert dancers despite having hardly ever danced when they were married.

The settings where dances are held vary as much as the locations of parties do. Clubs that are sometimes open to the public, like PWP and its commercial counterparts, can attract large crowds of all kinds of people. Their dances are often held in hotel or motel ballrooms, whereas church groups usually use the churches' recreation halls. Sometimes a small club reserves a large table at a night club, where members can dance not only with each other but with other customers. The environments range from modest to luxurious, and the music varies with the tastes of the majority of the members.

After a dance, it is acceptable and typical for two people who have just met to extend the evening by going out for a drink or coffee and dessert. More often, small cliques of old friends assemble at a favorite watering hole or eating place — or go somewhere to dance some more.

From all of the foregoing it is easy to see why the clubs of Single World provide an efficient environment to find dates and get a new social life going. Don't be seduced into spending all your leisure time and spouse-hunting efforts in Single World, however. Be sure to spend at least half your time in Real World pursuits such as adult education, sports, and cultural activities. Things go slower there, but you can and do meet people, date, relate, and — more often in that milieu — remate. The two worlds can be compared to the old story about the turtle and the hare, and you know which one won the race.

The same applies to travel. There's Real World travel with friends, family, and groups or organizations; and then there's Single World travel, which is worth looking into for the simple reason that singles travel belongs to Single World and provides many unique advantages. The next two chapters will tell you about them.

7.

Anchors Aweigh

"The Love Boat" television series, now in reruns, certainly helped to popularize the cruise industry, which was once largely the domain of the older, more affluent, and more sedate clientele. Today people from all social and economic backgrounds enjoy this unique kind of vacation.

ALONE OR WITH A GROUP?

Single people in particular have taken to the ocean waves in large numbers. A few take cruises on their own, which I think can be a mistake. You're traveling in a corner of Real World which is largely populated by couples, and you usually wind up the odd man or woman out. A good number of singles, on the other hand, sign up for nationally advertised singles cruises, which draw vacationers from all over the country. These have both advantages and disadvantages, which will be described. Another large number of singles go on cruises organized in their own areas, often by travel agents who are themselves single and members of singles clubs. I think these cruises are the best choice because of both cheaper rates and the opportunity to meet people you can continue to see at home. Many of the considerations which apply to cruises also apply to vacations at resorts, such as Club Med, which will be described in the next chapter.

CONSULTING A TRAVEL AGENT

I knew practically nothing about singles travel when I decided to take a cruise. I told my travel agent, whom I had picked at random out of the phone book, enough about my situation to get a good cruise recommendation. But I was fortunate. An agent with a good reputation who is a member of a singles club could eliminate some of the chance involved, or a single friend who has traveled a lot could be another good resource. Many single women either work full-time as travel agents or supplement their incomes by working part-time as agents or tour escorts. Those who are active in Single World know the places singles like to go, including the cruises favored by single travelers. They are also qualified to advise you where not to vacation — where others have not had a good time.

When asked, a few single people will tell their travel agents they are going on a cruise for "rest and relaxation" and really mean it. They want a real vacation for a change. On the other hand, most newly single people say their goal is simply to have a "good time." Sometimes they add, "If the right person comes along, well, fine." Translated, this means that they have their fingers crossed in hopes of finding someone they can relate to or maybe remate with; but if this doesn't happen, they'll settle for fun and games. They are best served by going on singles vacations sponsored by local agencies or singles clubs. These can be a better deal, since group rates are cheaper, and more importantly, many of the people you meet aboard ship live in your area, and a shipboard romance needn't end when the two of you step off the gangplank.

KINDS OF SINGLES PACKAGES

The singles packages put together by the national travel agencies are best suited for those singles who really mean it when they say all they want to do is play and stay single for the time being. Often organized out of New York, these tours are advertised coast-to-coast and draw singles from all over the country. Follow-up dating is thus both difficult and expensive.

Some cruises or resorts make it quite clear that they offer their clients the ideal opportunity for casual flings with people they will probably never see again. The very name of a resort like Hedonism II in Jamaica indicates what the people who go there want to pursue. An experienced agent can tell you about all kinds of playgrounds.

The easiest to sign up for, often the least expensive, and usually the most enjoyable cruises are organized by local singles clubs or club members. I prefer the group package deals because they're both less costly and more convenient. Usually you sign up at a club meeting, and all the arrangements will be made for you, including itineraries, transfers, and accommodations. All you need to do is pay your money and bring your clothes and your smile.

Don't go overboard (no pun intended) and buy a whole new

wardrobe. Casual clothes are what you'll see during the day, while dinner in the formal dining room calls for dressier attire. Women can wear either formal gowns or cocktail dresses to the Captain's Dinner, and suit coats and ties are usually adequate for the men. Most people I know use their existing wardrobe. When you book your cruise, ask for a brochure that tells you exactly what to pack.

A good cruise director will have your days packed with events, too. Bringing along a camera to record the events is always a good idea. A camera can be a wonderful icebreaker.

BREAKING THE ICE ABOARD SHIP

On a nationally organized singles cruise aboard the *Norway*, I watched a single fellow approach first one woman and then another while they were taking snapshots of the boat and the scenery. He good-naturedly volunteered to take their pictures against whatever backgrounds they were photographing at the time. Almost all the women said yes, glad for the opportunity to be in a picture they could show their friends back home. So he snapped away, and when he handed a camera back, he'd open a low-key conversation about the cruise, the scenery, or whatever, and volunteer to take a few more snapshots by the bow, the pool, the railing, and so forth. Later I noticed him having a cocktail with one of the women he'd met, dancing with another one, and talking on deck with yet another. By the second day, he was "going steady" for the duration of the voyage. I envied him.

I got acquainted with the camera operator (pun intended) by congratulating him on his successes. I asked if it didn't bother him when he was rejected by some of the women, as he sometimes was. He said it didn't; he was a salesman, accustomed to approaching prospects, and he knew that some would buy his product and some would not. To those women who weren't interested in pursuing a conversation, he nodded a friendly "You're welcome." There was no reason for either of them to feel embarrassed. He had only done a small courtesy. But if she seemed willing to get to know him, all the better. Attitude counts for so much.

I tried his technique and it worked. I pass it along because we need all the excuses we can come up with to get to know strangers without benefit of introduction. No matter that the real motive is that we find someone attractive and want to get to know him or her, we need some reason to start talking to a stranger — some shared experience or common interest. Offering to take a photograph is perfect. For that matter, any offer to help someone do something is an excellent icebreaker, not to mention an act of kindness. Making a friendly comment — on the beautiful seascape, the good (or bad) weather, the fine food, or the quality of entertainment — can also be quite effective. Nothing ventured, nothing gained.

BRUSHING UP ON OLD SKILLS

Playing cards is a useful social lubricant. What you play is up to you, but I've found that playing a passable hand of bridge provides entry into congenial groups wherever you happen to go. Bridge players aboard ship tend to gravitate around card tables for at least a couple of hours daily. Rather than engage in the ship's planned activities full-time, they'll fill some of their leisure hours with the challenging competition — and socializing — that bridge makes possible. Other enthusiastic card players do the same thing, and it's not at all unusual for several players — in a hearts game, poker game, pinochle game, or whatever — to discover they have more in common than just cards. Incidentally, bridge groups and other card-playing groups are found all over Single World. What's more natural than to start dating someone you get to know across a card table? I know people who have gotten married because of bridge (also some who have gotten divorced).

Besides brushing up on playing cards, be sure you know how to dance, at least fairly well. On any singles cruise or resort trip there will be dancing. Aside from the intrinsic enjoyment and exercise value, dancing is quite simply the best way to get to know the opposite sex. The first night of a singles cruise everybody will be invited to a party to help break the ice. In fact, there is dancing in the lounges every night both before and after dinner for the express purpose of helping the singles aboard to mingle and get to know each other. Even if you haven't had time to brush up on your basic dancing skills, the best way to improve is with practice, and you'll have plenty of opportunities aboard ship. You'll meet lots of people that way, and that's what it's all about.

A NATIONALLY ADVERTISED SINGLES CRUISE

Barely passable dancing skills were all I had when I boarded the *Norway* and nervously embarked on my first cruise — not just my first singles cruise, but my first cruise ever. By this time I had been divorced about a year, and although I had joined a singles club and begun dating, I was still very unsure of myself.

I had mistakenly always thought that cruises were too expensive for middle class budgets, which simply isn't true. I spent only as much as I customarily would for a week's vacation. The one-week singles cruise package I chose was sponsored by Gramercy Tours out of New York City. Air travel to Miami and transportation to dockside were included in the package. I wondered if there might be some additional significant charges, but there weren't any.

I checked in at the customs building and boarded my ship a little after noon. Everything went smoothly. The *Norway* was scheduled to sail at five o'clock, and since it would take a while before my luggage would be put on board and taken to my cabin, I decided to do a little exploring. I found that the *Norway*, like every large cruise ship, has a pool, several lounges, a main room used for evening entertainment, a gambling room, and a small boutique where you can buy items you forgot to bring with you (try not to forget much; these shops are very expensive). And, of course, there's the main dining room.

On the *Norway* our first-day luncheon was a buffet featuring a delicious turkey casserole along with tasty salads and sumptuous desserts. A little overfull, and a little overtired from my early morning flight connection, I went to my cabin, unpacked, and catnapped for an hour before the ship sailed.

Like most of the others, I was out on deck to watch the ship put to sea. With that bit of excitement behind me, I returned to my cabin and looked through the orientation kit supplied by the Norwegian Caribbean Lines. Be sure to examine your version when you take a cruise. Mine was filled with useful information, including a list of events scheduled for the first twenty-four hours. Thereafter we received daily printed bulletins describing all the events and entertainment.

ABOARD THE *NORWAY*

I learned from my information kit that a before-dinner cocktail party was scheduled for the Gramercy singles group. I left my cabin immediately and joined the thirty or forty people who were already assembled in one of the lounges. The Gramercy guide who greeted me was outgoing, pleasant, and articulate. A good-looking man in his thirties, he was just the sort of person you would cast for the role if you were a movie director. He announced that there would be unlimited free drinks for everyone for the next hour, and a few singles managed to down five or six drinks in the allotted time. Most settled for two or three. Then the guide gave us a thoroughly professional briefing on our cruise package, assigned us tables for our meals, and gave us instructions for contacting him with questions or problems. He possessed a remarkable memory for names, and in a very short time helped us to feel comfortable with him and with each other. The cocktail party was a good opportunity to mingle, loosen up, and get acquainted. Most of us were middle class, though a few had some of the trappings of wealth, and the group was not unlike various singles groups I had been with before. This introductory get-together had been timed to end some fifteen minutes before we had to go back to our cabins and get ready for dinner. After dinner there was to be another singles party, this time for all the singles aboard ship, including those of us with the Gramercy tour.

On returning to my cabin, I met my cabin mate, who had arrived late because of delayed travel connections. A pleasant Latin man in his early fifties, he told me his college-age children had urged him to take the cruise to "get away from it all." We talked briefly before dinner, and I found out he was a salesman for a large corporation with South American interests. He seemed to have everything going for him. He was handsome, obviously well educated and affluent, well built, and effervescent. He was friendly and outwardly cheerful, but nevertheless he seemed somewhat distracted and sad. I learned that he had been only recently divorced, and I could understand. I had passed through that stage myself — and was still passing through some of it.

Our fares were much less than they would have been if we had opted for single cabin occupancy. The company used a computer to match cabin mates by age and background, and this generally worked out well, although, with the cooperation of the tour guide, a few women did switch cabins.

GOOD FOOD, GOOD COMPANY

My cabin mate and I barely had time to get acquainted before going to the dining salon for dinner. I immediately felt that we would get along just fine, and we did. He was considerate and good company whenever we were together, though this was not very often. I stayed close to the Gramercy group, while early on he began to spend most of his time with a woman who was with another group of passengers.

The food aboard most cruise ships is everything the advertisements say it is, and maybe even better. Superlatives just can't describe how good it is. Unfortunately, you can have all you want, and many of us overextended ourselves during the first few days. We were offered steak, prime rib, lobster, shrimp, and a lot of tasty dishes with fancy French names. There was always a long list of appetizers to start with and an array of delicious desserts to finish with.

For the most part, we sat with our tour group, six to a table, three men and three women. There were two extra people in our group, but immediately following the introductory cocktail party, a newly formed couple requested and were assigned a table for two.

The three women at my table were office workers in their thirties and forties. They were friends back home in Chicago and liked to travel together, so they periodically splurged on a luxury cruise like the one we were on. The oldest woman, about forty-five, was outgoing, pleasant, and lots of fun. She had traveled extensively and was knowledgeable about any number of other cruise ships. Not only was she fun, she had come to have fun. The youngest of the women was quite pretty and loved to gamble. Unfortunately, she usually lost. The third woman was quite thoughtful, shy, and sensitive, yet very pleasant. I got the impression that she had recently been hurt.

One of the other two men at my table was about forty-five and worked in flood control out west somewhere. He tended to be a loner. The other fellow was about thirty, gregarious, and well traveled. You could tell he was out to make merry — and all the Marys he found along the way who were willing. He soon made good progress in satisfying his compulsion; he had come to the right place. Even though my singles tour group had disparate backgrounds, beginning that very first day we all became fast friends for the duration. Maybe people dance a little faster on a one-week singles cruise. In any event, we liked each other and hung around together exchanging gossip and good humor. We often sat together for the evening's entertainment and took our shore excursions together. I guess we looked like we were having fun, because outsiders occasionally asked to join our group.

Adding to the friendly atmosphere at my table was the wonderful personality of our waiter. Bryan was a born comic whose ready smile, sense of humor, and sunny disposition brightened everything and everyone around him, and we couldn't have asked for better service.

RECREATIONAL ACTIVITIES

Just about everything on the *Norway* was top-notch. The social directors (a husband-and-wife team) and their staff saw to it that our hours were filled with activities. Two or three different fun-filled activities competed for our favor just about every hour of the day. Overall, this was a classy ship. The *Love Boat* didn't have a thing on us.

Considering the temptation of three gourmet meals a day, not to mention the midnight buffets, I was more than pleased that the ship offered many excellent opportunities for exercise, along with a splendid orientation concerning health in general. If you feel you're ready for that health kick you've been promising yourself for years, a cruise ship is a good place to begin. Many a physical fitness program must have either begun or gained impetus aboard ship.

The *Norway* exercise program was labeled "Fit for Fun." Part of one of the decks was set aside for walking and jogging. The fitness program was exceptional, stressing the wellness concept and encouraging people to begin exercising in a prudent manner. Not only were we given instruction in calisthenics and aerobics, we attended lectures and saw films on improving muscle tone, flexibility, and strength, with an emphasis on cardiovascular health. Instructors demonstrated several fitness options, and we were warned against such pitfalls as overdoing it or choosing exercises inappropriate for our ages or fitness levels. Aerobic dance classes were offered for the young with physically young hearts and the middle-agers in excellent condition. We were shown how to gradually increase our pulse rates and respiration through simple steps and continuous movements and how to use slower movements to gradually reduce our pulse rates to normal. We were also taught how to measure our pulse rates and learned the ideal rates for different age groups. Separately, there was slimnastics instruction, which emphasized weight reduction and trimming the figure. Fat chance with those super meals on board!

The professionals on ship helped us formulate specific exercise plans which we could follow through on when we returned home. Obviously no one can get in good physical shape in only one week, but a motivated person could make a start. Those who did, and kept on pursuing a suitable fitness program back home, truly benefited from the cruise. I know I did. I didn't realize it at the time, but this would be the most valuable and lasting benefit I got from the trip.

The *Norway* also offered ping pong, shuffleboard, horseshoes, skeet shooting, and, of course, swimming. Many kinds of arts and crafts were available, and dance lessons were provided where the sit-down-and-watch crowd was encouraged to get up and go. If we felt like reading for a while, there was a library, and card players had no problem finding other enthusiasts in the card room — which also turned out to be an excellent place to meet people. So much was offered that there simply wasn't enough time to participate in everything that sounded interesting.

Suppose, on the other hand, that your main reason for going on a cruise is to relax. Suppose you've been working hard and have no desire to have your days jam-packed with activities, or suppose you're not emotionally ready to get socially involved. No one ever pushed us to participate in any of the activities. On our ship, as on most, there were many passengers who elected just to relax in lounge chairs and sunbathe, although many of them danced and lived it up at night.

ENTERTAINMENT ABOARD THE *NORWAY*

The one thing almost everyone enjoyed was the entertainment after dinner. Crowds jammed the huge main lounge every night to see the comedians, singers, and a splendid dance troupe — all of the caliber seen in night clubs in Miami, New York, or Las Vegas. The *Norway* carries enough passengers to afford the best, and everything was top-of-the-line, including the two theater presentations. *Hello, Dolly* played to a full house twice nightly for three days, and then *The Sea Legs Review* was staged for the rest of the week. Both were superb!

I tried to sample everything — sun, swimming, and other activities by day, and dancing in one or more of the half-dozen lounges before dinner and after each evening's entertainment. I danced and talked with our group into the wee hours. (Fortunately, I somehow summoned the willpower to avoid the elaborate midnight buffets!) I also looked in on the bingo, participated in the Fit for Fun events, and played bridge.

Besides all this, there was a honeymooners' champagne party, a special program for teenagers, several fashion shows, and, of course, gambling. A fully equipped casino had all the action anyone could want, and gambling lessons were offered for the novice. For the sake of my solvency, I passed.

SHORE EXCURSIONS

Every other day or so during our week-long voyage, we dropped anchor at a Caribbean port, and shore excursions were available for a modest additional cost. Our first stop was St. Thomas in the Virgin Islands, where the sight-seeing tour was especially worth the money. We circled the island in a rickety bus, stopping first at Blue Beard's Castle, a famous three-hundred-year-old structure that had been converted into a hotel. We enjoyed a splendid panoramic view of the harbor before continuing on to Rampoon Hill and Casey Hill, past the Pineapple Beach resort, and then on to Coki Beach. All breathtaking! We also visited Coral World, where, safe in an underwater observation tower, we watched divers hand-feed sharks and marveled at sting rays, barracuda, and giant eels as they swam past the thick glass windows. Finally, we were driven to the heart of town and encouraged by our tour guide to go on a duty-free shopping spree.

Another excursion choice available in St. Thomas was the Kon Tiki Tour, featuring a huge glass-bottom boat complete with band and three hours of unlimited underwater viewing and unlimited rum punch. We were also given time in St. Thomas to snorkel or go for a swim in the ocean, or go for a lazy walk on the beach.

With all the fun and games both at sea and in port, in the company of so many interesting new friends, and under the wing of the cheerful Gramercy escort, there was no way any of us could feel depressed or unhappy — that is, unless we were doggedly determined to do so. I must confess, though, that unlike the four subsequent cruises I took, there were moments when I came close.

EMOTIONAL BENEFITS

I went on this cruise not too many months after the trauma of my divorce. I was still hurting emotionally and still feeling down, and my self-confidence was shaky. The cruise, along with my other Single World activities, helped me begin my recovery. Nothing dramatic occurred, but when I got home I found it much easier to get out of myself and out of the house, to meet with people and enjoy new activities. There were still bad periods, of course, but they were milder and less frequent. Later still, I began to notice that I was emotionally comfortable much of the time and occasionally in a happy mood. In a few more years I could thoroughly enjoy myself doing things, going places, and being with people. I had never dreamed so much pleasure would be possible for me.

I think this all began at sea. One moonlit night while gazing at the ocean and the universe of stars, I found myself contemplating the world and my place in it, the successes I had known in my careers, and the failure of my marriage after so many years. I decided then and there to treat both Triumph and Disaster as the imposters Rudyard Kipling found them to be. I remember making a conscious decision that even though I would continue to care about people, I would never again take them — or myself — too seriously. I left Rudyard on deck alone with the stars and joined the group in the main lounge, where I spent the next few hours enjoying good entertainment, conversation, and laughter with my new Single World friends.

In retrospect, I don't think this cruise would have been nearly as beneficial or enjoyable had I not been with a singles group, if instead I had been one of the regular Real World passengers.

For the most part they were married and had another outlook and different interests. I would have felt awkward, and maybe even like an envious fifth wheel in their company. They seemed to be having a good time, but on their own terms — in another world I had once inhabited. Their conversation would have reminded me of the interests that were dominant in my past married life and made me feel worse rather than better.

I have always been shy about meeting people, and without the tour escort and the singles ambience of the group, I might well have had difficulty and spent a number of lonely, miserable hours.

The experience might have been a disheartening fiasco rather than a positive psychological turning point.

Because of my experience, I wouldn't hesitate to recommend a singles cruise (or tour) to help you break your social routine, get out of your emotional rut, and build a bridge from your old world to an exciting and adventuresome new one. I would advise, however, that you not go with the idea that you'll find a new mate. Rather, go on your singles trip with the idea of keeping an open mind and enjoying yourself. Take the tip from Kipling and don't take anything or anybody too seriously. Accept the fact that if all you get is rest, relaxation, and some emotional rehabilitation, you've still accomplished a great deal.

If someone really nice should happen along and an interesting interlude occurs, all the better. My guess is that about half of our singles group found sex partners. They were usually discreet, but gossip never takes a vacation — even on a vacation. There were those sudden absences and locked cabin doors and some good-natured kidding. On the other hand, some in the group had actually taken the cruise primarily to enjoy the good food, good entertainment, and relaxing ocean vistas. They too were well served. A minority, however, came looking for new spouses. They should have stayed home. The Gramercy tour guide confirmed my observations.

A WORD FROM THE SINGLES ESCORT

Earlier in this chapter I described the *Norway* cruise escort Gramercy Tours had provided and said that he was young, unmarried, articulate, outgoing, and handsome. He was also experienced and knowledgeable about his job, the tours, and the needs and desires of his clientele. While earning a liberal arts degree in history, he had spent one summer as a replacement escort on a cruise ship.

"It was a paid vacation, and it was great," he told me when I interviewed him. After graduating, he told me, he had taken a manager-trainee position in a large New York corporation but had eventually become disillusioned.

"What the hell am I doing here? I hate this whole scene," he recalled asking himself. He said he called his old tour boss on impulse and asked if he could get back on a ship as a tour guide, explaining that he wanted to change his lifestyle and do something different. Within two weeks he was aboard the *Oceanic*, and while at sea he got a call from New York asking if he could handle two more cruises over the next few weeks.

"That was about fifty cruises ago," he told me. "I've been having such a good time that I don't have any desire to quit. I've met a wide variety of people, not just those I'd normally deal with in New York. I've met Jamaicans, Koreans, Norwegians, people from Australia and Germany — almost every country: I've made a lot of friends and enjoyed it."

He described his job as helping people to get the most out of their vacations. This involved trouble-shooting any shipboard problem that might come up, giving advice and guidance, and offering side-trips that the ship didn't provide. He was an excellent facilitator. He steered us to the right places at the right times and almost always got us excellent seats for the entertainment.

I was curious as to whether he might have had a hand in facilitating anything in the boy-meets-girl department, and I asked him about it.

"What I don't do is find men for women and vice versa," he answered emphatically. "My groups are usually more women than men, about two to one. Sometimes the younger women will come up to me the first night and say, 'Well, where are all the guys?' I'll tell them, 'Remember all year long when you went out with your boyfriend and you went to a concert or the movies or dinner? Remember when your date kept reaching in his pocket to bring out that green stuff to pay the bills? That's where the men are, back home in Hoboken, broke, wondering just what you're doing while you're on this cruise ship.'"

I wondered if many people had found a Mr. or Ms. Reasonably Right on a cruise, so I asked: "How about people who are looking for a mate here, not just a date? The people who watch 'The Love Boat' and are looking for a happy ending? And what about you? Don't you want to ever get married? You must have had lots of chances."

"I think marriage is a fine institution for most people, probably all people," he replied. "I don't think I'll be sixty or seventy and not have somebody with me. It's nice to grow old with someone. I'm fully aware of that."

I waited for him to say "But ..." However, he thought for a moment and then referred to the spouse hunters. "I tell a woman, as tactfully as I can, that my job is not that of Cupid. In all other ways I try to make the voyage as enjoyable as possible. As far as I'm concerned, if you're looking for Mr. or Ms. Right, this is not the place. Back home, that's where to look. Here, even if somebody finds someone, there's only a week to get acquainted — long enough for a shipboard romance, but that's all. Sunday morning comes soon enough, and when it does, he goes back to California and she returns to Virginia. Once in a while I'll hear that a couple has corresponded after leaving the ship, but for the most part, passengers shouldn't expect too much after the trip."

"But lightning does strike," I persisted. Were there any people he knew who met aboard ship and later married?

He said he'd received two wedding invitations. "I believe one of those couples broke up after only three or four months, but the other couple, Jimmy and Diane, were made for each other. They were both from Tennessee, and they found each other the third day out. From that point on they were locked. Every time I saw them they were holding hands or snuggling. I think that one was permanent." He hadn't heard of any other marriages.

Did people, both men and women, often ask him to act as an intermediary to bring them together? "Yes, all the time." But he refuses and claims that almost all tour escorts also refuse. "Often people don't come right out and tell me to find someone for them, but they hint around.

"I had a woman on the *Skyward* a few months back, a nice lady in her mid-forties, very shy, very quiet, and very pretty. She said, 'I'm not asking you to find someone for me, but if you meet a nice guy, someone you might pick to go out with a friend, tell him I'm in my cabin and don't go out much at night, and if he'd like to give me a call and go out for a drink, I'd be delighted.'

"That night I met a guy who seemed to be okay. In his mid-forties. I told him, 'Listen, there's a gal in my group who seems kind of shy and quiet. You won't see her here on the dance floor, but if you call and invite her for a drink, I think you might enjoy taking to her.'

"Well, she called me at midnight screaming that I had tried to get her raped. This guy came down to her cabin, opened the door, looked right in, and said, 'Okay Baby, here I am.'

"I looked for him in the morning. 'What happened? What did you do?' I asked the guy.

"'You told me she was ready to go, a free spirit.'

"My God, man, all I told you was to invite her out for a drink!'"

An unhappy passenger is precisely what a tour director doesn't want. "On the other hand, I'm glad to do legitimate favors for people when I can, even though I know they're trying to make a connection. A fellow on this cruise, as a matter of fact, asked me within fifteen minutes after we first got together at the cocktail party if I could arrange his table assignment so he could sit with a particular woman. No problem. I did it for him."

Was there much bed-hopping on this cruise? "I've seen one fellow here operate. He wants his own little harem, which can be a mistake."

"Why?" I wanted to know.

"What happens, not so much on these Norwegian Caribbean

ships, but more on some other ships out of New York City, is that you get a lot of the New York-New Jersey-Connecticut fast runners, if you know what I mean. They go from woman to woman asking this one and that to go to bed. As big as this ship is, come Wednesday or Thursday it can seem very small. Back home, when a man or woman bar-hops and does the one-night stand routine, they're not apt to run into that person again. Here, the next day they'll probably come face to face at some function or other.

"I had a fellow named Danny once who tried to pick up three different women the first night out. They all turned him down. Each one of them had seen him in a tête-à-tête with the others. Well, that poor kid couldn't find anyone to even hold hands with all week long. He came to me on Wednesday and said, 'What's going on? How come all these other guys are strolling the decks with some cute gal and I can't even get a friendly hello? What did I do wrong?'

"I explained to him how women talk to each other. Ask one to go to bed and the others will find out. Most of the women on the cruises aren't out for one-night stands. The best thing for a man to do is take it easy. There are always more women than men on a cruise — good-looking women. When it comes to finding a sex partner, men have the advantage aboard ship."

I found myself thinking that impatience and ineptitude are the bane of the newly single, and so unnecessary. The only thing people need to do is position themselves where they can meet many members of the opposite sex, then simply be friendly and take it easy. Nature and the percentages inevitably take care of things eventually. Desperation and nervousness cause some singles to press too hard, as Danny did, and the tendency for others is to withdraw from the desperate.

Another fact of life is that normal people shun those who are rude or offensive, a condition that can be brought about by too much booze. The tour escort told me that the only recurring complaint he received was about abusive language at the table, and this was almost always caused by inebriation. On rare occasions the offender was so abusive that he was removed from the tour at the next port of call and his money refunded. More often, the group will ostracize the offender, and the person becomes uncomfortable and makes himself scarce.

"Mostly, though, people have a good time," the guide concluded, "and they often cruise again." I did. I went on four more cruises in the next four years. The tour guide gets a lot of letters and cards from people thanking him for helping out. I certainly sent him one.

CARNIVAL'S GOT THE FUN

The following year I took a cruise aboard the *Carnivale*, one of the cruise ships of the Carnival Cruise Line. That cruise and the three that followed were organized for singles by either local travel agencies or local singles clubs. Two were escorted by people I already knew. Some packages can be rather expensive, like those sponsored by the Adventure Travel Club, but usually they are not, catering as they do to singles from PWP and some of the middle-class commercial clubs.

The less expensive, locally organized vacations appeal to a broader spectrum of singles and, like the more costly trips, are lots of fun. You get to meet singles who live in your own backyard, so you can continue shipboard friendships and romances back home — a very big plus. My social life gained impetus after each of the four locally sponsored cruises. After all, the more people you know, the better your chances of meeting someone you like and find interesting. Beyond that, you soon build a solid support group of Single World friends and acquaintances — almost an extended foster family. The PWP chapter in Clearwater has been one such "family" to me.

The *Carnivale* cruise was jointly sponsored by members of the Adventure Travel Club and members of PWP and offered the same fun things to do as my *Norway* cruise, but on a less expensive and less elaborate scale. One advantage was that our tour guide was a popular member of both local clubs. An astute and personable woman we all knew and liked, she was every bit as helpful as the Gramercy Tours professional escort on the *Norway*.

When we stopped at adventurous Caribbean ports, our escort joined the fun on our shore excursions, which included sight-seeing, night-clubbing, and shopping. While the top-of-the-line *Norway* vacation was certainly worth every extra penny, the *Carnivale* package was a better value. I also got to meet (or know better than I did before) several women I later dated. In contrast, a single exchange of Christmas cards was the only follow-up to my nationally advertised singles cruise.

The Carnival Cruise Line has a television commercial featuring the slogan "Carnival's Got the Fun." It has. The *Norway* cruise and all the others I went on were fun, too. For that matter, I also had fun on all the locally sponsored singles vacations I took to resorts, foreign cities, and other playgrounds. Club Med and some of the others are described in the next chapter.

8.

Faraway Places

Singles who don't particularly care to cruise or who prefer a mix of both land and sea vacations have a number of options. Again, the best source of advice is a person from one of the singles clubs who owns or works for a travel agency. Again, the best way to go is with other singles from your community. The trip doesn't have to be long or costly; enterprising travel agents can take advantage of bargain opportunities and group rates to obtain surprisingly cheap accommodations. Moreover, your chances of meeting new people and deliberately entering or falling into a relationship are about the same whether it is a weekend trip or one of a week or two.

These close encounters of the local kind can even initiate events that will change the course of your life when you get home. One of these trips did so for me, so I'll describe that trip first. I'll also tell you how I escaped the prospect of a bleak, lonely Christmas by opting for a three-day AAA Christmas package. Finally, for those who want to take off by themselves for rest and relaxation or fun and games, I'll tell you what it's like to take a Club Med vacation.

LOBBY OF THE REFORMA

The trip that led to a meaningful relationship for me was an Adventure Travel Club sojourn to Mexico City. About thirty of us from three or four local singles clubs signed up for a long weekend package. The all-inclusive price was such a bargain that it was hard to turn down, and since the trip was widely advertised and promoted at several local clubs, it drew a wide variety of singles ranging from the fairly well-off to the struggling middle-class.

The trip would be the first for our tour escort, an enthusiastic, gregarious, and attractive Latin woman who had lived in Mexico City for several years before she was divorced and still maintained close ties there. This, we all thought, would be a blessing. It was, a mixed one.

On the appointed day we arrived at the airport early in the morning, some coming alone, others in small groups. We were in a festive mood, and our effervescent leader (also a born comedienne) quickly put everyone at ease, outsiders included. Soon there would be no strangers in this group, only friends and friendly acquaintances.

By now I had accumulated some singles travel experience, enough so that if I had been really attracted to one of the women, I would have made it a point to enplane right behind her so we could sit together. However, not seeing anyone who immediately caught my fancy, I decided to keep my options open. Actually, I didn't feel all that motivated to get involved just then — a reaction to a series of relatively brief adventures that had not been very emotionally satisfying. Though I was "between relationships" at the time, I was in no particular hurry to find someone, having resolved simply to go with the flow and see what happened. If I were to meet someone interesting, fine; if not, there'd be another time. This was a very good attitude to take to the high altitudes of Mexico City — or to anywhere else for that matter.

After an uneventful flight from Miami, we landed and were capably herded through the airport onto buses and deposited in the lobby of the Reforma Hotel in downtown Mexico City. The words "Lobby of the Reforma" would take on a special meaning for us that would later inspire gales of semi-hysterical laughter. This comedy began as soon as we got to the hotel.

The man who was to be our professional tour guide met us in the lobby and began to brief our tour escort. The rest of us shuffled around impatiently or found seats, because apparently we couldn't go up to our rooms until something was settled. We wanted to unpack, refresh, bathe, and get a little rest before dinner and the evening's entertainment.

Just when it looked like the quarreling and bickering, that is to say, the negotiations, had come to an end, an old Mexican friend of our escort breathlessly rushed into the lobby, greeting her affectionately and effusively. It seemed our escort had written him about our trip, and being the friend he was, he had decided to show us the city himself. He hadn't come unprepared; parked outside the hotel was a minibus with a driver. His offer came as a surprise to our escort, to the contracted tour guide, and to our group — not that we had any idea what was going on.

The three of them were soon in a tumultuous argument. Even though most of the rest of us couldn't understand a word of Spanish, we watched intently, hoping to get a clue. As a group, our heads bobbed from one combatant to the next as though we were at a tennis match tracking the ball back and forth. Somebody could translate a word every now and then, but our attention was held by the fervent excitement and the hope that we could soon go up to our rooms. The escort's friend was determined to give us a tour of his city, and the professional guide insisted, rightly, that it was his job and that he would conduct the tour whether anyone went along or not — so that he could get paid.

The escort apparently joined her friend in trying to persuade the professional guide, but in the end — about an hour later — a compromise was reached. There would be two tours, one led by her old friend with the minibus and the other by the professional guide. The first night we all opted to go with the escort and her friend, first to dinner and then for a tour of the night life. This choice was our first mistake.

There was soon more confusion. Some within our group thought that the Reforma Hotel was not at all up to their expectations, even though the accommodations were certainly adequate. The package we bought was a terrific bargain, and bargains seldom involve luxury. Even so, four members of the group were adamant and determined to be put up in a better hotel. This took still more time. Finally, everything was settled to everyone's satisfaction, and we could all go up to our rooms. We hurriedly cleaned up, having been told to come right back down to the lobby to meet and board the minibus with the escort and her friend. The latter was determined to show us the Pink Zone downtown before taking us to dinner, and he had made reservations for us at a "real Mexican restaurant, the kind tourists never get to see."

The escort's ambitious plans for an early start on the evening immediately went awry. A goodly number of the group took the time to bathe leisurely and to rest a little before getting dressed and coming back down. This meant that those of us who had hurriedly gotten ready, as instructed, had a long wait in the Lobby of the Reforma, alternately grousing and laughing about the fiasco. We nevertheless really liked the escort, who had often entertained us in her home, and we collectively decided to grin and bear the ever-exasperating tragicomedy. So we bit our tongues and said nothing when she finally joined us, herself quite late. (But then, she was always late.) Someone remarked, "I've been here all day and what have I seen? The Lobby of the Reforma." We all laughed. That was the start of it.

The group was finally assembled and we boarded the minibus, only to learn that the escort had forgotten the name of the hotel where we were to pick up the four dissidents who had sought more luxurious accommodations. The only solution was a trial-and-error search of all the good tourist hotels in the Pink Zone, up one street and down another. "Could this be the one?" "How about that one? " It was close to ten o'clock before we found them, and by the time we got to the "good Mexican restaurant," we were all half-starved. It was a good thing we were.

The restaurant was large, and earthen pots accented the decor. The food, the prices, or both must have been good, because the place was crowed with locals. However, most of us liked the familiar Tex-Mex style of Mexican food served in the Southwest and in most other American "Mexican" restaurants, and this was quite different. I found the food to be much too heavy and didn't enjoy it, but by this time I wasn't in a mood to enjoy anything.

After dinner, tired from the long, frustrating day, we boarded the minibus gratefully expecting to be taken back to our hotel for a good night's sleep. But our leaders had other plans, and we headed for a nightclub. At least it was a good club, and the show was first-rate. At 1:00 A.M. we again boarded the minibus, all of us definitely anticipating our comfortable beds, but our pro tem guide insisted on showing us still more of the city's night life, and we were driven to a square crowded with revelers dancing, playing music, and hawking all kinds of merchandise. It was all worth seeing, and much of the merchandise was surprisingly cheap, but most of us were in no mood for celebrating or shopping, and we eventually prevailed upon our escort and her friend to take us back to the hotel. Just as we were entering the hotel, someone exclaimed, "I never thought I'd be glad to see the Lobby of the Reforma again." Everyone broke into hysterical laughter, stopping only long enough to agree to meet in the lobby at 8:00 A.M.

There was a rebellion in our ranks as we sleepily straggled into the Lobby of the Reforma the next morning, and the escort could no longer marshal all the troops to follow her and her friend into the minibus. Some of us felt that we had paid for and were thus entitled to the services of the professional sight-seeing guide, whose tour we had ignored the day before. Thus about half of us went with the hired guide rather than risk whatever another minibus tour might have in store. The other half went with the escort, either because they were reluctant to hurt her feelings or because they were late coming down to the lobby. We learned later that the escort's group left almost two hours late to see "the real Mexico City that tourists miss out on" and spent most of the day being driven out and around the city on an extended shopping tour.

The rest of us were quite content to see the sights that tourists do get to see, together with an experienced and interesting commentary in passable English. In the morning we saw the Presidential

Palace, an archaeological dig in the heart of the city, a famous downtown church, the beautiful campus of the University of Mexico, a fashionable neighborhood of the rich, and the site of the 1968 Olympics.

We enjoyed a leisurely and delicious lunch and were bused to a state-regulated arts-and-crafts shop stocked with quality goods at reasonable prices. Our guide was well qualified and had the knack of allowing just the right amount of time at each stop. Our last stop was famous Chapultepec Park, which included recreational facilities and three museums. These interested me, and I decided to return the next day and go through them at a more leisurely pace. As we reboarded the bus, I remarked to no one in particular, "Chapultepec and its museums look like a great place to spend the day. I'm coming back here tomorrow."

I was surprised to hear someone in our group ask weakly, "Do you mind if I tag along?" The voice belonged to a woman who had been sitting next to me during part of the tour. I had known her casually from a bridge group we both attended regularly, and I also remembered seeing her a few months before at a PWP dance class. A fellow member of the Adventure Travel Club, she was easy to talk to, well informed, good-natured, and good company. Looking back now, I realize she had been tagging along at every stop. We had shared a table for four with another couple at lunch, and she had graciously offered to help me find gifts for my daughter and daughter-in-law at the arts-and-crafts store. I liked her in a casual way, as a nice person, but hadn't really thought all that much about her.

Why I had never before thought of her as a potential date, I don't know. She was certainly nice enough in every respect. She seemed noticeably relieved when I answered, "I'll be glad to have your company."

Months later she confessed that she had needed to summon every last ounce of courage she possessed to ask me if she could come along. She said that if I had turned her down, however politely, she would have died on the spot.

It was late afternoon when we returned to the hotel. The group on the minibus would be late, as usual, though we were scheduled to reassemble at six o'clock sharp for transportation to dinner. Fortunately, we had prevailed upon the escort and her friend to take us to one of the fine Mexican restaurants that tourists do get to see. A few minutes before six, half our group was gathered in the Lobby of the Reforma ready to go, but, of course, we had to wait for the other half. When we finally boarded the minibus, we made the best of it, joking and laughing about perpetually warming the seats in the Lobby of the Reforma.

We got to the Los Morales Restaurante over an hour late. By

then the place was jam-packed and the tables reserved for us had long since been given to others. Once again our escort and her friend began an animated discussion in Spanish, and somehow the maître d' was prevailed upon to squeeze in more tables along one wall to accommodate us. This took a good deal of time, and we were famished. Fortunately the meal was so good and the atmosphere so congenial that we were mollified, even happy, by the time we had finished dessert.

After dinner we took a walk around the premises for a little exercise before boarding the minibus and — so we thought — going back to the hotel for some much-needed sleep. Close to midnight, it had been a long day, especially for the loyalists who had ridden all day in the minibus. Some of them desperately craved sleep, and we all needed it. But it wasn't to be, not yet anyway. The escort and her friend said that in order for our visit to be truly memorable, we simply had to top off the evening at a super night club. A show of hands indicated that a slim majority was still game and would opt for the "truly memorable" evening at a "super night club" which apparently everybody in Mexico City was raving about.

The Salon Belvedere, located on top of the Continental Hotel, was featuring a tremendously talented headliner — a singer, violinist, and exotic dancer all wrapped up in a gorgeously packaged woman named Olga. Her troupe included a magician, a comedian, and a chorus line. The escort's friend had apparently been there before and knew everyone, and he conspired with Olga to set up one of the men in our party. At the appropriate point in her act, Olga dragged the man up onto the stage to become the object of a few jokes, and then she had him put on a grass skirt and hula dance with her. He did quite well and she complimented him for being a good student. The crowd started chanting *beso, beso* (kiss him), and knowing what it meant, he chimed in too and soon led the crowd like a cheerleader He handled things well and managed to escape without making a fool of himself; the Mexican audience was delighted. Maybe our hero did so well because he was stone sober. A teetotaler, he always ordered *una botella de agua sin hielo* (a bottle of water, no ice). He never did get that kiss.

We all had a great time, but it was close to 4:00 A.M. when we finally got back to the hotel, completely exhausted and faced with the prospect of only a few hours of sleep. But the experience had been worth it.

At the appointed time the next morning only a few of us straggled down to the Lobby of the Reforma to meet as planned. Miss Tagalong was there on time, and so was I. We ate a roll and had some quick coffee before hailing a taxi to visit the Chapultepec Park and its museums. Later we learned that there had been another long wait in the lobby before the loyalists assembled for another minibus tour. Their plan was first to do a bit of sight-seeing and then visit the private children's school owned and operated by the family of the escort's friend. It was agreed that we would all meet at the San Angel Inn for Sunday dinner at 2:00 P.M.

Tagalong and I spent a pleasant time briefly visiting all three of the museums in the park. My idea was to walk through them all quickly, see what was there, and then go back another time, since it was simply impossible to do the museums justice in one morning. The world-famous anthropological museum demanded and got the lion's share of the brief time available to us. Then we walked through the museum of contemporaneous art, and finally practically ran through the museum of modern art. We grabbed a cab and raced __ all cabs in Mexico City race __ to the San Angel Inn, which was in another part of town. I suppose we didn't want to risk the ever-so-slight possibility that the minibus tour would get there on time.

The headwaiter showed us to the long table that had been reserved for our party, and Miss Tagalong and I sat down and waited, and talked, and waited. By the time the minibus arrived — a full two hours late — we had really gotten to know each other. The poor people from the minibus were exhausted, really too tired even to enjoy dinner. Somehow the escort and her friend had managed, all in one day, to show them "everything worth seeing in Mexico City." The woman who dragged herself into the seat next to me had looked half-dead in the lobby that morning, and now half of the other half was in question. She hardly touched her food, took no part in the conversation, and almost fell asleep.

After a delicious meal, the minibus took us all back to the hotel and we went up to our rooms, where we packed to catch our flight back the next morning, and fell asleep exhausted.

We flew back tired, but with the feeling that we had had a wonderful vacation — despite the delays, the snafus, and all the waiting in the Lobby of the Reforma. Perhaps the sense of camaraderie that developed was in part due to all the foul-ups, which we could now look back on with good humor. As I sat on the plane with Miss Tagalong beside me, it seemed that a lot more than just three days had elapsed. No longer were there any strangers among us, and a few, including Miss Tagalong and I, had sown the seeds that would develop into close relationships back home. Others had laid the groundwork for some dating. We all made friends, and I still highly value the many friendships I made in those four short days.

The hectic and exhaustive pace of the Mexico City trip is not typical. It was an informal trip, put together by amateurs for friends and led by one of us in conjunction with a singles club connected indirectly to a travel agency. "Regular" package tours, put together and guided by professionals, almost always run smoothly and on schedule — but without the atmosphere of fiasco and fun that our escort and her friend made possible. They wanted the trip to be a memorable one for us, and it certainly was. No way would I have missed it!

A MERRY CHRISTMAS

There are times when either by choice or by necessity you might just want to get away from home to help you navigate through an unhappy period of time. Specifically, I'm referring to holidays when you may feel that everyone else is going to be happy enjoying friends and family, but you anticipate being alone and miserable. With Christmas fast approaching, this is exactly where I found myself one year after my divorce.

I had business in the local office of the American Automobile Association (AAA) about then, and I noticed a travel brochure describing an inexpensive three-night Christmas sojourn to Jupiter, a town on the east coast of Florida. The package included an evening at the Burt Reynolds Theater with tickets to a play. I knew that Christmas spent alone would be a difficult time for me, and I wanted to get away from my everyday environment, do something different, and meet some new people. I signed up.

We travelled by bus. Besides giving us a bit of a travelogue en route, our tour guide gave all the unaccompanied people the opportunity to meet each other by suggesting that we change seats after each meal or rest stop. This worked out well, and by the time we arrived in West Palm Beach, the majority of us who were traveling alone had had the opportunity to make a number of friendly acquaintances.

Upon arrival, we settled into excellent accommodations and enjoyed a meal, and the next day we visited points of interest in Palm Beach and West Palm Beach — all on schedule and all made enjoyable by our very capable guide. The highlight of the trip was, of course, the evening at the Burt Reynolds Theater, where we saw the outstanding musical *Man of La Mancha*. The tour was very well-run throughout, and we were given just enough time at the various points of interest to enjoy ourselves yet not feel rushed. The four days filled out my holiday season and helped me over the emotional hurdle of an anticipated bleak Christmas.

CLUB MED

Among the get-away packages popular with single people are the one-week vacations sponsored by the Club Med chain, which operates over one hundred resorts worldwide. One fee covers almost all the costs involved, including transportation from hub cities. Though the resorts are not limited to singles — some cater to families — those that attract singles can be great fun, depending on your age, interests, and tastes.

After you obtain a Club Med brochure and before you decide which resort to go to, by all means call their 800 telephone advisory number to obtain additional information. The brochure makes all the resorts sound fantastic, and many travel agents will tell you only what you want to hear in order to get your booking. I was under the false impression that all the Club Meds were pretty much alike, and I thought it would be great to visit Cancun, Mexico. I thus ended up at what turned out to be one of the world's water sports capitals, catering primarily to young singles in their twenties and thirties. Upon arrival I saw mostly young athletes sporting patches from sporting events all over the world, and the club actually awarded Olympic-style medals for various competitions in an Olympic-like ceremony at the end of the week.

The food was super and the nearby sight-seeing outstanding, though, so I came out okay. I got a gold medal, of all things, for my prowess in the dining hall, a silver medal for paying attention to the sight-seeing guide, and a bronze medal for shopping for gifts to take back home. What I really deserved were booby prizes for all the sports events, which included swimming, snorkeling, scuba diving, water-skiing, windsurfing, and sailing. Aerobics was popular, as were volleyball, basketball, and tennis. All kinds of exercise equipment were available in a gymnasium.

Better I should have stayed home? No, not at all. A lot of what you get out of any vacation depends on the attitude you take with you, but much more also depends on the quality of research you do when deciding where to go. I shouldn't have stayed home, but I should have done my homework better, principally by consulting a knowledgeable single or travel agent I knew and trusted to select a particular Club Med vacation that was best for me. All this notwithstanding, I did have a good time on the trip and I learned a thing or two.

YOUR POCKETBOOK

Perhaps you may be thinking at this point that what has been said about singles travel is all well and good, but where does the average person get the money to pay for it all? First, I should point out that all the trips I've described were taken over a period of five years. Also, I habitually took advantage of tours and trips offered at bargain group rates by local singles clubs, and I always accepted a roommate or cabin mate to contain costs. I know of many who cruised four to a cabin.

Ending unhealthful habits also saved me a great deal of money. For one thing, I quit smoking. I had smoked three packs a day for decades, and this alone saved me roughly a thousand dollars a year. Moreover, I quit drinking, and this too resulted in a large savings, maybe another thousand a year. (I also noticed that since I quit I made more friends who either didn't drink or drank very little, and thus I saved money on my dates.) I discovered that putting aside some bad habits not only did my body a world of good, it did my wallet a world of good, too.

Besides your wallet or purse, take along a good attitude and an open mind. You can have a good time even if you don't find what you're looking for, be it Mr. or Ms. Reasonably Right or a casual fling. If you're looking only for the latter, the fastest results are obtained not in Real World or Single World, but in Casual World, the risky world of singles bars, dating services, and personal ads. We'll take a look at each of these in turn in Part III.

9.

Looking for Love in all the Wrong Places

Middle-aged singles who spend most of their free time in singles bars may be doing so for one or more of three reasons: (1) they have become habitual drinkers; (2) they have experienced exceptional difficulty in Real World or Single World meeting and relating to the opposite sex; and (3) they want quick and easy sexual liaisons with as many different partners as possible. The lifestyle of these "regulars" or "veterans" contrasts with that of singles who go to bars from time to time for a few drinks and some dancing. These "occasionals" or "amateurs" are not card-carrying members of Casual World, only visitors. However, at any future time, especially one of crisis following a broken relationship, the occasionals may turn into regulars — that is, they slide out of Real World or Single World and begin to socialize exclusively in the riskiest corner of Casual World — the bars.

A knowledgeable observer once remarked, "Sometimes we tell ourselves we'll go to a singles bar tonight just to get out of the house, and that we'd be happy just to find someone pleasant and attractive to talk to, and maybe dance with a little." He goes on to say, "Then, of course, there is sex. Most of us like sex, and we may be looking for sex, but we are not looking for AIDS, or herpes, or what have you. Our motives get complicated, but one of the problems is that after a few drinks things become deceptively simple and clear. One of the great lines from a country and western song is 'The girls all get prettier at closing time.'"

The men get more handsome, too, but the physical and emotional risks stay the same, even for those of us who are middle-aged and perhaps less impetuous. The physical risks — social disease and crime — have no respect for age, and as we get older the emotional hurts may not seem as severe, but they often seem to last longer.

HERNANDO'S HIDEAWAY

A singles bar is any bar that is generally known by the patrons to be a place where men (usually alone) and women (usually in pairs) go to drink, dance, and search for liaisons. Any bar to some extent qualifies, even the neighborhood taverns and the bars primarily patronized for entertainment, but a real singles bar will have a reputation as such. Most singles bars cater primarily to the younger crowd, but there are some which are popular with middle-agers. Hernando's Hideaway (not its real name) is a good example in my area.

Hernando's Hideaway caters mostly to middle-class, middle-aged patrons. It approaches being upscale, and it is known to most singles in the area. The bar is not billed as a singles bar, of course, but as a "Restaurant and Lounge." It is on a main street in a busy commercial neighborhood and has a large, well-lighted parking lot. You can order dinner if you wish, and there is a dining room, but most singles don't come to eat.

There is a band every night of the week and dancing. The band is competent, but nothing to rave about. The musicians are experienced, middle-aged men who can play just about anything and are used to getting lots of requests. Except for the drummer, they all play at least two instruments. You suspect that most of them have part-time jobs during the day. The dance floor is medium-sized. Most of the patrons like to dance, but it's not the main reason they're there.

On a typical night Hernando's will start to fill up between five and six o'clock. This is the first shift, the happy hour, when dinner dates are arranged. This is almost exclusively a singles shift, the women coming in pairs or small groups and the men coming alone or occasionally in pairs. Couples will usually not drift in until after dinner, when the band starts. The singles who can't arrange dates during this first shift will sometimes have a few two-for-one drinks, go home, eat and change clothes, and come back. Others will eat in the dining room or make do with the hors d'oeuvres at the bar and sit tight (pun intended) until the second shift, which starts about nine o'clock with the band's first set.

The second shift will include a few couples, many who drifted in after dinner for a few dances and a few who came because they love to dance, but primarily it is a singles crowd. Most of the patrons are in their forties and fifties, and the sex ratio is fairly even. A few tables may be pushed together to accommodate groups from singles clubs, but most of the patrons spend little time sitting and make use of the small tables and the bar just as places to put their drinks.

THE PLAYERS

Without a playbill giving the actors' backgrounds, a casual observer can nevertheless sort the cast of singles into various categories. The most important and perhaps most obvious distinction aside from age is the veterans versus the amateurs. The amateurs include both the new singles and various other singles who don't come in very often. Typically, about half of the patrons would qualify as amateurs. The veterans have clearly been here many times before, or to bars just like it. They either know the bartenders and barmaids well by now, or they will get to know them quickly — they are not shy. The veterans usually know each other, too, but they don't usually congregate for long or make plans with each other. It is each man for himself.

The amateurs, on the other hand, are often easily identified by their shy, hesitant actions and nervous behavior, or occasionally, especially if newly single, by their exuberance (free at last!) to pursue their fantasies of sexual adventure in Casual World. The veterans may drink twice as much, but the amateurs often show the effects more. Sometimes a veteran will bring along a newly single friend to teach him or her the ropes — often the case with women who work in the same office. A glance will tell you which is which.

There are other ways to tell the veterans from the amateurs. You won't often see an amateur male with gold chains, expensive rings, and carefully styled hair. Amateur women will often have elaborate, easily mussed hairdos and their clothes will be either a little too frilly or sexy or not frilly or sexy enough. Another tip-off can be the degree of attractiveness. Very few veterans are extremely attractive, although they know how to make the best of what they've got. Highly attractive men and women usually don't need to frequent the bar scene, unless they become drunks, in which case they don't stay attractive very long. On the other hand, very few veterans are unattractive. They would not have much success in this one-glance-and-you're-out world. The average veteran — man or woman — would rate about six or seven on a scale of one to ten.

Drinking styles also reveal a lot. Men who drink extra-heavily — except for an occasional amateur — usually won't be seen in Hernando's Hideaway. They usually hang out in neighborhood taverns or drink at home. They wouldn't be too successful picking up women, anyway. The same is not necessarily true for women who are heavy drinkers, however. They can usually get lots of free drinks, and if they are not repulsive, they can usually get a man to take them home for more drinks and whatever. The veteran male will pace his drinking. He knows how much he can hold and still perform. You won't see him drinking shots with a beer chaser. You may, however, see the veteran woman drinking shots if she is a serious drinker — or more likely, something mixed strong or straight on the rocks, which seems more ladylike — and you won't usually see her with a fancy colored drink with lots of fruit and a little umbrella. Incidentally, the veteran who doesn't smoke cigarettes is a rare bird indeed. The veterans are almost always pretty good dancers, sometimes very good. This is of course an essential part of a man's bag of tricks. The veteran women don't have to be good dancers, but they usually are anyway.

Perhaps the best way to sort the veterans from the amateurs — apart from actually talking to them — is to observe their facial expressions. Veteran men are usually smiling, and at the same time seem cool and collected. They positively reek of assuredness (and sometimes of cologne). They are, after all, salesmen. (A surprising percentage of them actually make their livings as salesmen.) Many of the veteran women also have an aura of assuredness, and many seem hardened, even cynical.

The only sure way to distinguish between the singles bar regulars and the occasionals is by talking with them, assuming you'll get straight answers. When asked if they come to Hernando's often, some will say, "Only once in a while." That could mean they come every other night or that they usually go to the bar down the street. An accomplished veteran knows how to tell you pretty much what you want to hear without having to outright lie.

By this time you may be asking, "What difference does it make if they're veterans or whatever?" None, really, if you know what to expect, and many of us do know what to expect. We walk into the bars with our eyes wide open, having heard many sad stories about bar liaisons from friends, and maybe having had a bad experience or two in the bar scene ourselves. Maybe we've read the book or seen the movie *Looking for Mr. Goodbar*, commiserated with someone whose younger sister got V.D. from a handsome vacuum cleaner salesman she met in a bar. Every morning people wake up to find themselves with strangers they would never had bedded had they been sober.

Sometimes we may find ourselves sitting at the bar next to an unemployed reprobate or tramp someone just threw out of the house after three months of drinking and bickering and lies. Maybe the ex-couple first came into each other's lives at Hernando's Hideaway, where one squeezed the other's hand and whispered sweet nothings. We know what to expect. But here we are again, back at Hernando's, because we are lonely, and because, we tell ourselves, "You never know when Mr. (Ms.) Right will happen along," when the best we can realistically hope for is Mr. or Ms. Temporary, and what we'll probably end up taking home is Mr. or Ms. One-Night Stand. Possibly when we do get home and look in the mirror that night, we'll see before us Mr. or Ms. Struck Out or, worst of all, Mr. or Ms. Drunk Again.

THE CURTAIN RISES AT HERNANDO'S

The players at the bar and sitting at tables examine each other with practiced glances. The men are deciding which women they will move in on, and in what order. Simultaneously, the women are judging the crop of available men, mulling over which ones might be acceptable. The veterans can accomplish all this without seeming to look anywhere. They have made careers of judging people at a glance. Automatic updates and reappraisals are constantly fed into their seemingly oblivious mental computers. The regular players all have eyes in the backs of their heads.

Many of the decisions about who shall end up with whom seem to be made even before the players have spoken to each other. Miss Cute knows that Mr. Tall will soon come over to chat and ask her to dance. She will dance with him and let him buy her a drink, but she has her eye on Mr. Bald. She knows, though, that Mr. Bald will first approach Miss Smile, who is younger and more attractive. Chances are, though, that Miss Smile will eventually reject Mr. Bald because she has her own eye on Mr. Tan. Mr. Bald knows Miss Cute is available to him, but he has to give Miss Smile a try first any way. But wait, Mr. Tan has just walked out alone! That changes everything! And so it goes.

Perhaps the saddest thing about all this is that many of the veterans feel absolutely compelled to go home with somebody — as a last resort, almost anybody. They cannot bear to spend the night alone. They may tell themselves that they want the sex, that they are on the make, or that they are just playing around until the right guy or gal comes along. The fact is, they can't stand being alone. An acquaintance once confided (bragged) to me: "I've picked up dozens of women in bars since I got divorced. I could find out something I really liked about all of them, and I told them so. I told most of them — in bed — that I loved them, and I meant it. I love women. I love sex. I hate to sleep alone." He hates to sleep alone; he hates to be alone.

THE DIALOGUE

The singles bar mating game usually calls for the man to make the first verbal move. More often than not, the woman has encouraged him by sending nonverbal signals. They've exchanged glances and perhaps smiles, and he feels comfortable with the thought that she isn't going to turn him down cold. He'll ask her to dance and end up sitting next to her. If all goes well, she'll allow him to enter her space and lean close to her. Before long she may touch his arm, maybe while leaning forward and laughing at something he said.

Highly popular and profitable books have been written which suggest "lines" that are supposedly guaranteed to work. Eric Weber's *How to Pick Up Girls* has sold thousands of copies by advocating what psychologist Chris Kleinke, in a thoughtful study of the phenomenon, has termed the "cute-flippant approach." According to Kleinke, Weber's cute approaches, such as "Do you think I deserve a break today?" and "Your place or mine?" are mainly used by men who unconsciously are trying to protect themselves from the threat of rejection. These lines turn off a lot of women, and once considered humorous, they now seem inept and trite, if not insulting.

Kleinke instead recommended the use of innocuous questions such as "What do you think of the band?" or "Where are you from?" He also advised a direct approach at appropriate moments: "You're a great dancer. I'd like to get to know you better." As I have said before, I don't think it makes a whole lot of difference what is said at first, so long as it is not crude or insulting. The person will be interested or not, and most of the time what you say won't make much difference.

Anthropologist David B. Givens, another student of the bar scene, also advised against the cute-flippant approach as well as the so-called macho approach. In advising against coming on too strong, he explained, "Courtship is tentative, ambivalent, an exchange of signs over a period of time." He described the five stages as (1) Getting attention, (2) Moving closer together, (3) Conversation, (4) Sexual arousal, and (5) Resolution, a term he says he uses for "euphemistic reasons." Successful resolutions occur when the two strangers leave the bar together to go to one or the other's apartment or to a motel.

ROMANTIC COMEDY OR GREEK TRAGEDY?

It depends. The outcome varies with the individuals and how they act. There are those, especially younger players, who perform the scene intermittently or for relatively short periods of time in which they do enjoy a romantic comedy of sorts. The fortunate or perceptive become bored or disgusted with the meat market and leave while they're still ahead of the game — often having found a mate there or elsewhere.

Playing the singles bar pickup game regularly, though, is for the middle-ager like playing Russian roulette. Nothing more than a romantic encounter may occur the first time, or the second, or the third, or the thirtieth, but those who keep pulling the trigger with the pistol to their head sooner or later come to grief. It's human to think it could never happen to us, and in fact, it might not. But then again, it might. The following item appeared in a local paper recently:

> A twenty-two year old Tampa man was arrested and charged with sexual assault of a woman he allegedly met at a bar, according to the Hillsborough County Sheriff's Department. [Name omitted] was arrested at noon after the victim escaped and led police to his home. Lieutenant...said [name] met the woman at a local lounge and took her to his house, where he allegedly handcuffed her to a bed and assaulted her. [Name] is being held without bail on sexual battery and false imprisonment charges.

Although this sort of outcome may be relatively rare, there is another kind of tragedy. It is the tragedy of getting involved with someone you don't really know and ending up in a relationship which is destructive but hard to bring to an end. Loneliness all too often skews our judgment. A friend writes:

> I've been divorced for about fifteen years. I've spent about half that time, off and on, living alone. What would eventually happen would be that I'd get very lonely and start going to bars. Sooner or later I'd meet a woman who liked me, and we'd get something going. I didn't have to think the world of her, because I figured it would just be a temporary situation with some good sex. I was never much for one-night stands, so I always ended up living with them — or they with me — for a year or so until I found some excuse to call it off. The last woman I picked up in a bar stayed with me over a year, and she never worked a day. She had a list of addictions and other problems as long as your arm, and she ended up costing me thousands of dollars. Maybe she was the worst in a lot of ways, but the others were all inappropriate, too. Now I go to singles clubs and support groups.

An affluent woman I know has had similar experiences. She prefers younger men and is pretty good at picking them up in bars when they are down on their luck. They'll move in with her, entertain her in bed, eat her food, spend her money, and drink her whiskey; but as soon as they find a decent job or another woman, they'll provoke an argument and move on to greener pastures. Each time she swears it will never happen again.

The cold fact is that singles with long-standing problems tend to repeat their destructive behavior over and over until they themselves change in some significant way, by eliminating or ameliorating their negatives (see Chapter 3).

LES MISERABLES

Remember, a person needn't be obviously drunk to be an alcoholic and at times can even seem funny and likeable. Likewise, people with other serious long-standing psychological or emotional problems also may superficially seem to be normal and likeable. The best place to find both types is in the bars. It sometimes takes years, even decades, for alcoholics to either stop drinking and regain their health or become nonfunctional and eventually die. Meanwhile, their lives become a carousel of carousal — round after round of heavy drinking, pickup, heavy drinking, arguments, loss of job, heavy drinking, physical ailments, heavy drinking, auto accident, heavy drinking, DWI, jail, new job, heavy drinking, pickup, arguments, heavy drinking...

Elizabeth Horman, a social worker and author of a series of excellent book reviews in the PWP magazine *Single Parent*, has found from her work experience that most of the people who came to her professionally were having difficulty adjusting to some major transitions in their lives. More often than not, it was either divorce or the death of a spouse. Her experience showed that only a few of her clients had had a history of serious emotional problems prior to their divorce, but in a high percentage, "alcohol played a major role in shaping their lives or in creating their current problems."

Anyone who has recently been divorced or widowed has enough adjustment problems to cope with; no additional problems are needed. If you decide to go to singles bars to pick up strangers, chances are you might have some fun, but you will also have some less-than-desirable, maybe devastating experiences. Ann Landers gave out good advice to a reader who wrote in that she had dressed well and gone to all the classiest bars in town but was unable to meet any first-rate men. Ann's advice: "If you want to catch trout, don't fish in a herring barrel."

Those who are determined to visit Casual World for fun and games would be better off using the dating services. How? With great care! The next chapter tells about it.

10.

Taking a Chance on Love

Seldom do people admit to using the so-called dating services, but many do use them, discussing their participation only with those they meet in this manner. Why do they subscribe? Most say that they don't have much time for dating in the first place and that their situations make it difficult for them to find suitable dating partners where they work, live, and play.

If you subscribe to a dating service, you will doubtless meet people who really do have very little time to participate in Real World and Single World activities, where the sexes can and do meet and get to know each other over time, date, and enter into relationships. It is true that some people are crowded by time, but it's also true that people usually find the time to do what they really want to do. There is little doubt that many of the dating service clients are pursuing a casual lifestyle in this manner simply because they prefer it to the bar scene.

You will also come across a minority who naively use the dating services in hopes that they will find Mr. or Ms. Reasonably Right, and if they are really desperate to marry, they will sooner or later sign up with an agency that is careful to call itself a dating service but implicitly represents itself to be a "mating service." Lightning does strike, and on rare occasions people do find each other through those means, but more often they get badly hurt, both emotionally and financially. (The mating services are of sufficient importance to be treated separately in the following chapter.)

The dating services simply constitute another corner of Casual World, a better alternative to the singles bars, and principally a place for non-serious players to seek to engage in fun and games. Many upwardly mobile young professionals seek to avoid entangling personal relationships that might impede their progress up the career ladder. Having decided to pursue a casual lifestyle, at least for the time being, they make use of the dating services as a simple and easy means of satisfying their physical and emotional needs while avoiding commitments. A serious disadvantage of prolonged reliance on the dating services for such purposes is that those who practice relating to the opposite sex only on a superficial basis — revolving around drinks, dinner, dancing, sex, and "next!" — may sooner or later find it difficult to relate to anyone in a nonsuperficial way.

WHO USES DATING SERVICES?

The dating services are not limited to busy professionals. The yuppies aside, subscribers will include:

1. Those who are nice, decent people and potentially would make good marriage partners but have been unsuccessful elsewhere in finding a match. They date and keep their fingers crossed.

2. Those who have become disgusted with the singles bar scene or have suffered from really bad experiences in it.

3. Those who are afraid of people and too timid and shy to give Real World activities or the singles clubs a good try. (Some would have succeeded had they only forced themselves to keep going.)

4. Those who have been active in the singles clubs scene for years but have not been satisfied with the results and are now seeking new ways to meet people in hopes of eventually entering into a relationship or finding a spouse.

5. Those who are afflicted with alcohol, drug, or food addictions, or have serious emotional problems. Many of them are desperate, terribly isolated, lonely, impoverished, and in poor physical health. They enroll as an act of desperation, hoping against hope that some savior will magically materialize.

Everyone who subscribes to the mainstream dating services will find that quality varies and there is no really good way to know ahead of time which services will provide a reasonable number of desirable dates. The different subscribers have different backgrounds, goals, and expectations, and everyone having the money to pay the fee usually is accepted, though attempts at screening are claimed and in some cases (often half-heartedly) actually made. Nor is there any useful method of determining which agencies are more cost-effective than their competitors; you simply pay your money and take your chances. It's best to subscribe to a service which promises nothing except to put you in touch with other singles who share some of your interests, and you're safest if you subscribe to one that has been around for a good while. Remember that people are reluctant to admit using dating services, so recommendations from friends are hard to come by.

SIGNING UP FOR A DATING SERVICE

Dating services advertise in various singles publications, in special-interest magazines, and in the yellow pages (usually under Dating Service Bureaus). To get the specifics about cost and how to sign up, you simply write or call and they'll take it from there. It's a good idea to sign up with an agency for the minimum period at the least cost and see what develops. If you like the results, you can then sign up for longer periods, usually at bargain rates. Simply try another agency if you are not satisfied with the kind of people you meet or the number of referrals.

In common with the singles bars, this method of finding dates puts you in contact with strangers and involves a degree of risk. Unlike the bars, however, you can at least exchange letters, speak to the prospects at length on the telephone, and discuss each other's backgrounds and interests. Your dating selections can be made with a clear head after you hear what they sound like — and in the case of the video services, see what they look like. Moreover, you have a much larger pool of prospects to choose from than you normally find in a bar, and you avoid the tendency to pick up someone on impulse when the hour gets late and you've had a few drinks.

With the dating services, therefore, you are in a position to make deliberate and intelligent selections. If you later find upon contact that the person is unsuitable, you can always extricate yourself politely without worrying about where your next date will come from. A good dating service can provide many more referrals than most people can handle. For this reason, you are in a good position to exercise care and minimize the risks involved.

While it is unlikely that you will meet Mr. Goodbar through prudent use of the dating services, it is also unlikely that you will find Mr. or Ms. Reasonably Right. Remember, this is Casual World, and though all kinds of people sign up for dating services, the one thing that most of them have in common is that they are mainly looking for some laughs and an evening of casual diversion. If you do meet someone you really like, don't get excited and call your preacher. The fact is, the frequent casual encounters many subscribers enjoy are all they want — and in some cases, all they are capable of sustaining emotionally.

There are some dating services which specialize according to personal interests and can put you in touch with music lovers, art lovers, book lovers, those interested in various sports, and people with other interests. Sometimes dating services advertise in the classified sections of special-interest magazines.

It is a good idea to offer a prospective date only your telephone number and not your address, and it is prudent to arrange your first meeting at some public place — perhaps a coffee shop for lunch, or for coffee at another convenient time. The less the obligation, the easier it is to break off cleanly if it is immediately obvious that the two of you are a poor match. If after talking to a prospective date for a good while on the phone you think he or she sounds particularly promising, meeting at a restaurant for dinner might be appropriate.

When you decide to meet in a public place, be sure to describe yourself, mention what you will be wearing, and agree on precisely when and where you will meet. You can add a Hollywood touch by planning to identify each other by carrying books of a particular color, wearing a blue flower or red tie, or whatever. However you meet, if you sense that something is wrong when you come face to face, simply abort the date immediately by politely saying that something came up unexpectedly and you must leave. If the person is simply not your cup of tea, go through with a short meeting so as not to callously hurt his or her feelings.

PROCEED ONLY WITH CAUTION

The responsibility for screening your referrals ultimately lies with you, regardless of what the agency people say or promise to do. Although referrals from one dating service on the whole may be better or worse than those from another, inevitably there will be some referrals from all the agencies who are simply not for you.

Some highly disturbed people are good-looking and come across as charming. Late in 1987, a man was convicted of robbing and murdering a woman he had contacted through a dating service. Some years before, the nation was shocked and its attention riveted for weeks by the string of murders of young women committed by Christopher Wilder. His ploy was to scout the shopping malls for young women whom he lured with the promise of high modeling fees. He was caught because he had subscribed to a television dating service, and the nightly TV news repeatedly broadcast his video from the dating service. Wilder also frequented singles bars and could have been encountered anywhere in Casual World.

Sometimes alert observers can see clues that steer them away from the emotionally troubled. At other times this can be difficult, as in the case of Wilder. Dr. Gary Moran, a psychology professor at Florida International University, described rapist-murderer Wilder as a narcissistic sexual psychopath, but also had this to say in a newspaper interview: "The world is full of people who are borderline narcissistic psychopaths. Go to any singles bar in Miami and you'll find a whole damn room full of these people."

Your chances of bumping into sick people are probably greater among singles bar regulars than among dating service clientele, but with the dating services there is still a risk. Anyone already involved in picking up strangers at singles bars might just as well try the dating services as a somewhat better, clear-headed alternative for engaging in Casual World's arena of fun and games — much of the time just a playpen consisting of dinner, bed, and breakfast.

A LOOK AT SOME REFERRALS

For those who feel circumstances warrant giving dating services a try, the kinds of experiences they can expect to encounter are included in the remainder of this chapter and in the next. The first experiences are those of a "yuppie" living in the New York City area; a television dating service in Florida is described next; and the tribulations and exploitation of those seeking spouses through a "mating service" are reported in the next chapter.

I recruited Mr. Friendly, as I overheard one of his lady friends call him aboard the *Norway*, to sample the New York City dating services for me. He was the fellow passenger and amateur photographer I met on the cruise and got to know and like so well (and envy so much), and he showed a great deal of interest in this book after granting me an interview concerning Single World as he knew it. I asked him to research some of the dating services for me because he was good-looking, affluent, articulate, personable, and on the way up — obviously the kind of man most women would consider attractive. They certainly did aboard ship.

Apparently Mr. Friendly was equally successful on land, reporting back that in general he enjoyed the experiences in the two dating services he tried. Both services were inexpensive but provided him numerous good referrals, with only one bad experience in the lot, and it was more of an embarrassment and a trial than a real problem. After using the services for a few months, he sent me tape recordings describing his experience.

The first agency required an interview, which took about fifteen minutes after filling out an application setting forth his interests, hobbies, and preferences in women. Within a week they had a date for him, a "school teacher, tall, attractive, and a very nice person." Things went well. "On our first date we went out to dinner and had a good conversation. I was impressed by her and we came back to my place afterward. The second date she invited me over for dinner and put on a beautiful spread. We dated a couple of times after that, but I got involved with some other people and that ended that. A nice experience."

His second referral was quite different. Remember now, we are visiting Casual World:

> We went out once, just before Christmas. She wanted to fix me up with someone else and told me, "I've got this friend for you." I said, "Oh, you mean we can't see each other again?" and she said, "I think she'd be better suited for you."
>
> I forget her friend's name, but she was a wild little thing. She was out of her mind. It seemed like as soon as I saw her, she wanted to go to bed right away, which was fine with me. I went out with her several times. Then one day her mother called, said she was looking for her, and asked if she was over at my place. Well, she wasn't, but shortly afterwards she did show up. I decided she was a little immature. I felt I didn't want to be bothered seeing her anymore because she was a hassle, and I didn't want mothers calling me for their daughters. I prefer dating older women.

The third date from the same service was also primed and ready to go: "She came wearing this big hat. As a matter of fact, she came to my house on the first date, and I went out with her maybe a couple of times more. That was about it. She was attractive and fairly intelligent, and I really had no complaints about her. There were a couple more referrals from that agency, and overall I would say that for the money the experience wasn't bad."

His experiences with the second dating service were similar:

> This dating service is in New York City, but they are also national and have offices throughout the country. I found some of their ads in semi-sophisticated magazines. One read, "Single? Alone? Call us"; another, "Single? Meet that Special Person. Call Now." That agency was also inexpensive and their application contained blanks for phone number; sex; age; and whether you were single, divorced, widowed, or legally separated. They also took your weight, height, race, religion, and ethnic background and asked the applicant to indicate those he was willing to date, for example, Catholics, Jews, and non-religious people. Other questions related to one's occupation, hobbies, whether you have any children, if you smoke, and if you drink. Finally, the application contained a subjective area inviting you to "tell us more about yourself in a few paragraphs," and the last entry was "tell us more about the types of people you would like to meet — or avoid meeting."

Within three weeks, seven referrals came in the mail. Mr. Friendly entertained himself deciphering the numerical codes the agency used. "If you get the gist of how to read the code number, you can tell how old they are, anyway. For example, one girl is coded with the number 733-100-90. Well, the 7 means she is a white female, the 33 means she is 33 years old, and I'm not sure what the 100 means, but part of the zip code is also there, so it is all computerized."

The first referral he got from this second agency was the awkward one mentioned earlier:

The first woman who called turned out to be awful! Just awful! She lived in the next Long Island county, about twenty-five minutes from me. She called first, because she must have gotten her mail the day before I did. Anyway, she said, "I got your name through the agency." I said, "Fine, tell me more about yourself," and she began by telling me she was a registered nurse. One thing should have made me cautious about dating her — her voice. She spoke in a loud, grating tone that was uncomfortable to listen to. But we made a date.

When I went over to pick her up, I saw that she looked like Miss Five-by-Five. Jeez she was fat, and homely to boot! I mean she was awful! I sat down for a few minutes and tried to make some conversation. There was a piano there, so I said, "Who plays the piano?" and she said, "No one, it's just there." I said to myself, oh boy, this is going to be a long evening. What do I do? Do I pretend I'm sick and get out of here quick? But I decided to go through with a short date.

I took her down to a Howard Johnson's nearby, but there was a crowd of people there and a line fifteen or twenty minutes long. It's one thing to be ashamed being seen with a person, and I wouldn't have minded just being seen with her. What really bothered me was her loud tone of voice, which I found obnoxious. We were standing in line and I asked, "What are your hobbies?" She said, "HOBBIES? MY HOBBIES ARE READING AND KNITTING." Just about everybody turned around and looked, and I knew I had to do something. I figured the only thing I could actually do was either get her the hell out of there fast or else talk constantly so she couldn't get a word in edgewise. I decided to make some excuse and take her to dinner down the road where nobody ever went. I said, "Look, let's go down to this other place. I know we can get to eat real quick, and I'm hungry." So I got her out of there and we went to this diner.

I'm not kidding you, but the way she ate was awful! What manners! She kept her mouth all the way down to her plate. When it was time for dessert, she spent the longest time looking at the menu, trying to decide. She was studying the dessert list like a scientist would study a diagram of an atom. I decided to go to the restroom while she finished her dessert, so I could come back about the time she was done, pay the bill, and get the hell out of there. When I came back, I said, "Let's go. I'm really not feeling well," or some other god-awful excuse. I paid my bill and took her home. On the way, I asked her how much she weighed. She said one hundred forty pounds. Now, if she was one hundred forty pounds, I weigh ten pounds! Finally, I dropped her off, and that was the end of her — the end of an awful experience.

From then on, however, he felt that the dating service did fine by him. Here are some of his thumbnail sketches of the women he went out with:

[Ms. A] She was a very nice girl, about 5'4", 120 pounds, a biologist at a major hospital in New York City. We had dinner together, but I never called her back because she was located really too far from where I live, and I guess dates were kind of plentiful at the time. I had so many I didn't know what to do with them all. But she was nice.

[Ms. B] She was a personnel director and a very nice girl, well educated and well situated. We went out about two or three times, but there was some guy she had been seeing before, and she decided to stick with him. In the process, she fixed me up with a girlfriend she thought I would get along with, but we didn't hit it off.

[Ms. C] This girl kept calling me a lot, so I figured, well, this is the type I could easily score with, and I was getting kind of horny because I hadn't made it with [Ms. A or Ms. B]. She lived only about thirty minutes away from me, so I brought her home for the afternoon. She was admiring my wine rack and my stereo and my record albums and kept telling me about one of her old boyfriends who couldn't understand why she was a nymphomaniac. And I thought, Holy Mackerel! I'm going to move right in on this! I'm not wasting any time! So I was in bed with her in five minutes. Gosh, she was good! She was fantastic! I took her out a couple of more times, but she was really an airhead — didn't have much upstairs. She was some kind of hospital assistant. She was tremendous in bed, though.

[Ms. D] She was an attorney and real smart, but she was homely. I went out with her only one time. She was about 5'7", a nice girl, just not my type. I think she spent too much time in the books at law school and not enough developing the social graces. She was clumsy in her way, and she was a boring conversationalist.

[Ms. E] She was what you would call an intellectual —

anyway, very intelligent with lots of education — kind of cute, too. She was small, about 5'3", and weighed 100 pounds. She lived in Manhattan and had a Ph.D. She would talk on and on about medieval poetry and other things I never heard of. I mean I thought I was intelligent, but after I got through listening to her, I felt ignorant. Anyway, she was living with some guy at the time she dated me, also a Ph.D. I guess they had intellectual discussions in bed at night. Anyway, they were still living together, so I brought her over to my place one afternoon. But I didn't get anywhere with her, that's for sure. She basically told me that I wasn't smart enough for her, which maybe I wasn't. She was the type that when she would see some bird fly by, it reminded her about some passage in a poem written in the 1600's. She wasn't my kind of girl, and I wasn't her kind of guy.

[Ms. F] She was a knockout! Big breasts! Boy! Her personality was a little hard, maybe a little tough in a way. I took her out three or four times, and we really had a ball. One of the reasons I decided I didn't want to see her any more was that she was on the take all the time. I like to see a woman, on the third date, possibly the fourth, make some gesture of reciprocation, you know, especially if you have taken them out for expensive dinners a couple of times and maybe spent a hundred or so. You'd think they could at least invite you over to dinner sometime.

His overall impression of the women referred to him was good. "The dates from that agency were nice people, except for that first one. Everybody else was generally truthful about the way they represented themselves. I really thought it was an excellent adventure, and overall, my experiences were good."

A TELEVISION DATING SERVICE

The dating services which cater to the more mature have a more difficult time coming up with satisfying referrals. Most older subscribers have more than a passing if-the-right-person-comes-along interest in remarriage or are at least seeking a long-term relationship. There are agencies which seek to find suitable referrals along these lines, but finding a first-rate Real World mate with whom to live happily ever after is extremely difficult in the transient, superficial byways of Casual World. Many try, few succeed.

A conscientious effort to offer a service along these lines was made by a social service worker who migrated to Florida from New England. Herself divorced, and convinced that there was a demand for a good television dating service, she paid a consultant's fee to a video-dating concern in New England to learn how to set up and operate her own service.

The technique she adopted involved making her new clients comfortable by seating them on a sofa, offering them a glass of white wine or a soft drink, and explaining her service and interviewing them. During the interview she carefully checked them over for "acceptability" in order to "weed out those we don't think will do well." Those she discouraged from signing up were "mainly older women, because I know there won't be many suitable dates available to them, and there's no sense taking their money." (It should be noted that most dating service operators are not bothered by such scruples.) She also dissuaded the "grossly overweight and homely," because "it's sad but true that they aren't chosen."

She asked prospective clients to fill out a questionnaire concerning their backgrounds and tastes to help her decide which videotapes to show which members. Then they moved to a comfortable den to make the videotapes, and she conscientiously helped the clients show themselves off to best advantage in the five to ten minute videotapings. Her clientele mainly consisted of men and women ranging in age from the late twenties to the early fifties, and a sampling of half a dozen showed them to be upscale, employed, alert, attractive, eager, and aware. However, after about a year of operation, the agency went out of business. No known marriages had occurred.

DATING SERVICE TURNOVER

Because some unscrupulous operators promote dating services that are scams, and because "escort services" are often just fronts for prostitution, it is sometimes difficult for dating services to advertise in local newspapers, although this would probably be the best way for them to obtain clients. The *St. Petersburg Times* refused to accept advertising from the television agency described above, and this certainly hurt her business. She could have failed, however, despite her professional qualifications and long experience as a social services counselor, because of keen competition. Maybe she was lacking in business experience, or possibly she closed down voluntarily after she herself found Mr. Reasonably Right through her own agency.

Often singles searching for a Mr. or Ms. Reasonably Right of their own are motivated to start new singles clubs, dating services, or singles publications with this purpose in mind. The enterprises tend to fold after their quests either end successfully, become tiresome, discouraging, or too expensive or time-consuming — or if the originator happily adjusts to single life and pursues other interests. This particular dating service might have failed because the operator conscientiously eliminated large numbers of applicants she knew she could not help. Other agencies are not nearly so scrupulous about turning away desperate, unhappy souls who are willing to pay their fees but whose chances of finding dates are very slim.

Most of the regular dating services do in fact deliver the service that intelligent subscribers might expect from them, namely, to put the clients in touch with other singles they must personally screen in order to come up with a number of people they can date casually. The dating services also offer hope for the very outside chance that Mr. or Ms. Reasonably Right might come along — a hope that tends to evaporate with the experience of dating a succession of referrals.

There is a minority of services which promise more, much more than they can deliver: that they will find you a mate. They don't specifically promise this in their advertising for fear of lawsuits, but the ads certainly do lead the willing and gullible to think so. They follow up with a high pressure sales pitch appealing to the emotions and longings of the lonely, the isolated, and the desperate. During this sale/interview, usually in your home, they pass themselves off as matchmakers who will surely find someone for you. The promises they make are always implied and verbal, tailormade to appeal to eager ears hungering for words of hope for companionship and support. These promises to find a mate are never expressly set forth in a written contract.

Worst of all, in contrast to the relatively modest cost of most regular dating services, the ones that imply they are mating services are frightfully expensive. They do not hesitate to exploit their victims, usually women in their forties, fifties, and sixties who can ill afford the exorbitant fees, as we shall see in the next chapter.

11.

Fools Rush In

Whenever a dating service implies it is in a position to put you in touch with the love of your life for a fee — usually a hefty fee — run do not walk to the nearest exit. Typically, such rarely fulfilled promises are made verbally in the comfort of your home by a salesman skilled at forcing expensive written contracts onto the lonely, the isolated, the miserable, and the scared. I call such dating services by what they purport to be: mating services.

ONE MEATBALL

A newspaper headline reads "Matchmaker fails to find 'rare type' of eligible gentlemen," and the story relates why a Florida judge ordered a dating agency to refund two hundred fifty dollars and court costs to a fifty-nine year old woman. The agency had contracted to introduce her to at least three single men meeting her qualifications ("knowledgeable, considerate, understanding, and cultured") within a year's time. However, the agency sent out only one man, whom she apparently considered a meatball, reneging on the contract and making it possible for her to be among the few ever to recover their fees. Had the agency sent out two additional referrals, it is probable that the service would have been home free, and the woman out in the cold.

While the newspaper account used the term "matchmakers" in its story, the agency itself was careful only to promise introductions. Nor will you find a category labeled "Matchmakers" in the yellow pages of the telephone book. Such operators are fearful of being taken to court, so they list themselves as "Dating Service Bureaus," and as such they are mixed in with the regular dating services. Usually they feature slightly larger ads than the others, however, and they throw in a reference or two about screening, safety, and respectability. The regular dating services tend to have shorter ads containing fewer, if any, assurances. Either type may utilize the free 800 telephone numbers, but a clue to whether you are dealing with a dating service or a mating service is that the latter may try to arrange an interview in your home, whereas the former is content to have you fill out an application and send your fee by mail.

THE $200 HAMBURGER

A local woman in her early fifties reported on the merits of such agencies to a group she belonged to. She had telephoned an agency in the yellow pages that claimed to have been in business for a while and indicated it was respectable, and an appointment was made for a representative to come out to her house to interview her — actually for a salesman to come out, sign her up, and collect her money. He first offered her contracts for several months costing eight hundred dollars, but she pleaded poverty and prevailed upon him to make his final offer of one month's service at the minimum fee of two hundred dollars. For this she was supposed to receive three referrals.

Only one man called. He talked to her at length over the phone, arousing a suspicion that all he was interested in was obtaining a free housekeeper. In fact, more than once he asked her if she liked housework. Except for the fact that she had already paid her two hundred dollars, she would have turned him down out of hand and refused to see him. But against her better judgment, she did agree to meet him at a hamburger place he suggested so they could at least get a look at each other and talk for a while. No sooner did they meet than she could tell that he was completely unsuitable — in fact, "awful." She wryly told the group that it was the worst — and most expensive — hamburger she had ever had.

There were no other calls, and she didn't bother to call the other "gentlemen" referred to her, having been so disappointed by the first one. She hadn't gotten her money's worth, but what she had gotten was quite sufficient.

MY EXPERIENCE

When I began my field research on the mating service described below, I immediately found that most of the subscribers were lonely, frightened, and unhappy middle-agers dreading the specter of having to live into old age in isolation or without significant companionship. Clients came from all age brackets, but were mostly women in their late forties, fifties, and sixties. The minority of younger women in their thirties or even twenties appeared to be prompted by desperation; some had economic motives, others wanted someone to help them cope, and a few were looking for fathers for their children.

Some had sampled the singles clubs but withdrew hastily out of fear of rejection or because they were timid; others had spent years in them but found they could not find dates or relates in sufficient quantity or quality. Others were refugees from the singles bars who had either become disgusted with them or had fallen heir to a really bad experience. A few had wandered in from expensive dance studios, having found only dance partners, not the dating partners they sought. A minority were affluent; many were in dire circumstances. Some in their fifties or early sixties were retired; others were living on alimony or inheritances.

In short, I mostly found the lonely and isolated or the older, war-weary veterans of years of neurotic boy-girl combat in every theater of Single World and Casual World, many of whom were simply sick of it all and wanted to settle down with someone — almost anyone. The majority seemed to be without intimate friends and were emotionally or geographically distant from their relatives — more or less all alone in the world.

Included in this mix of mating service clientele I found a minority of solid people who have their acts together and have a good deal to offer, not necessarily financially, but in terms of character, values, and personality. I estimate the number of women I met belonging in this category to constitute maybe twenty percent. The dozens of women I questioned estimated that the number of decent men they had encountered through the mating service constituted no more than one or two percent.

Since most subscribers were in desperate emotional straits, they were vulnerable to the skillful sales pitches and empty promises. With an end to loneliness in sight and marital bliss in reach, even the financially pinched found the means to scrape up several hundred. In return for signing a binding contract, various numbers of referrals were received monthly. A woman usually got two to five referral slips a month, but these seldom produced more than one or two dates or face-to-face meetings — often none. If necessary, payments could be arranged to finance a contract after a down payment.

Most of the women I met were bitterly disappointed with the entire experience. While lightning can strike anywhere, and most agencies can indeed point to a few "successful" matches, most efforts to find a mate in this manner left the clients further down the emotional and financial scales than before, feeling more hopeless than ever.

"WHEN I GET FLEECED"

After I returned to St. Petersburg from my cruise aboard the *Norway*, I subscribed to the Get A Mate dating service, not knowing that, only a few days before, the *St. Petersburg Times* had published an in-depth exposé on them, masterfully researched and written by Thomas French. Even without this knowledge, though, my initial contacts with the agency had aroused my suspicions. However, I did want to describe a mating service in this book, and I figured there was an outside chance that I would meet' someone interesting. Besides, I was somewhat reassured by the fact that Get A Mate advertised itself in the yellow pages as a member of both the Greater Clearwater Chamber of Commerce and the Suncoast Better Business Council. Today they omit those claims and simply advertise that their "clients are screened," that they offer the "safest way to meet people," and that they are "100% confidential." The ad also assures the prospective clients that "loneliness is unnecessary."

I was discouraged with the results I was getting and learned why when one of the women I was dating brought out the newspaper exposé. Across the top of the article she had written in ink, "When I get fleeced, I get fleeced!" To my surprise, the service continued to flourish, despite the newspaper's wide circulation in the Suncoast area. However, I began to get referrals from other Florida cities, indicating that Get A Mate was advertising more widely. The lead for French's exposé read:

> The promise beckons. It goes out in television and newspaper advertisements to elderly widowers who spend their days alone inside trailer homes and to young women who pass their nights making small talk with strangers before a bar.
> Loneliness, these people are told, can be beaten.
> All they have to do is reveal their hearts and open their checkbooks to Warren V. Nicholson, the president of "Get A Mate" Dating Service.

French learned that in return for an open checkbook the clients, according to the agency's sales manual for employees, should be assured of "fulfillment and success" in two areas, "to remove loneliness and to find a mate." These assurances were unequivocally made to me by Nicholson himself during the interview in my home. He made his sales pitch and pressed me for his money then and there, in the process assuring me that it would be no problem for me to find a spouse through his agency within six months to a year. French's article continues:

> But some people who have joined Get A Mate and

some who have worked there, including a past president,
say that Nicholson's promise is hollow. They complain that
Get A Mate exploits its lonely clients...

When prospective customers are interviewed, their
conversations — including answers to intimate sexual
questions, such as whether they are willing to engage in
oral sex — are tape recorded. Get A Mate salespeople are
told to assure the clients that the tapes are confidential and
will be heard by no one else.

Reading this, I recalled being amazed during my interview with
Nicholson — his tape recorder quietly whirring away — that he had
the gall to ask questions that if answered could easily be used to keep
people from complaining or suing. What surprised me even more was
that some of these desperate, lonely people, having decided to go the
last mile in this effort to find someone, had indeed answered such
improper and embarrassing questions. To them Nicholson was an
authority figure in a position to grant their heart's desires, and they
looked upon him and his promises with such hope and longing that
they were simply unable to refuse to answer such wild questions.

My suspicion that Nicholson was entirely capable of using the
taped answers to embarrassing questions to intimidate those with
subsequent complaints was borne out by Nicholson himself when the
Times interviewed him:

But Nicholson says he would be willing to use the
tapes in court if necessary, and he even offered twice to let a
Times reporter hear a tape. He said the reporter could
"listen to any tape." When asked whether the tapes are truly
confidential, Nicholson said, "You can split semantic hairs if
you want to."

This was only one of many misrepresentations, among them the
fact that Nicholson once advertised that Get A Mate was licensed by
the state. It was not; no state agency in Florida licenses dating
services. Another false claim was that Nicholson's ads boasted that
no complaints had been filed against Get A Mate at the local Better
Business Council. In fact, eight complaints had been filed.

Since there is no licensing, regulation, or supervision of any
kind, the field is open to the worst kinds of misrepresentation. According to French, this applies to Get A Mate in spades.

And, though Nicholson tells prospective customers
that he screens his clientele because he does not want ex-
felons in his service, court and corrections records show
that he is an ex-felon himself.

In fact, Nicholson — who has served time in prison for
negligent manslaughter and armed robbery — concedes
that he would not qualify as a client for his own service.

Even though Nicholson himself would supposedly be ineligible to sign up for Get A Mate because of his prison record in three states, he nevertheless feels he is qualified to be the agency's president because, according to the article, he has "studied loneliness both in the classroom and among his clients and...knows how to help people fight it."

Like French, I was impressed with Nicholson's mannerisms, speech, and ministrations that made me think he possibly was once a clergyman.

Though Nicholson says he is not trying to sell religion, he talks...with the calm, deliberate intensity of a preacher delivering a familiar sermon. Indeed, his three-piece suits, the carefully-paced rhythm of his words, the accent left over from his home state of West Virginia — all give Nicholson the aura of a Sunday morning gospel orator.

Like a minister, Nicholson propounds the virtues of marriage. His message is simple: "Loneliness is the number one killer in the world. The best cure for loneliness is marriage." Apparently he is something of an expert, having been married and divorced five times himself.

What can be seen as a hint of cynicism on the part of Nicholson — and probably many others like him in the field — is evident when the *Times* quotes him as saying, "You can meet the nicest man in the world or the nicest woman in the world [and] sometimes your familiarity with them breeds contempt." Nicholson is further quoted as saying, at another time, "People are so phony and plastic — and I hate to say that because I'm in the people business."

How effective was Get A Mate in helping people find mates? Nicholson claimed that the Get A Mate promise was fulfilled for "many" and made much of a few times his clients did get together. Two of them, an elderly Clearwater couple, said they joined Get A Mate to fight loneliness after their spouses died. They didn't want to have their names published, because they didn't want their children to know how they met, and perhaps they also didn't want anyone to know they had gotten engaged on the day they met. The now-married couple said they were grateful for Get A Mate. "It's already cut and dried...like going to the store and picking out a new suit," said the sixty-six year old man. His wife was also happy: "I was choosy about dating anybody. I'm not going to throw myself away, even if I am sixty-one."

Apparently, however, Nicholson's claim that many of his clients find mates is a gross exaggeration. One former Get A Mate salesman cited in the *Times* believes that such marriages as may occur happen because "it's like throwing mud against a wall; you figure some of it is going to stick." He asserted that the primary basis for referring people to one another was their age rather than the psychological format

Nicholson claimed he used to match his clients. The salesman said that any success any particular couple might have enjoyed was "pure luck." His derogatory remarks were confirmed by Nicholson's ex-wife, whereas another salesman sided with Nicholson.

In my own extensive experience with Get A Mate referrals, I heard nothing from the women but criticism of the agency — without exception. Not once did I come across a woman from among the dozens I talked to or met who spoke favorably of the quality of the referrals or was at all satisfied with her investment — quite the opposite. The general complaint was that they received only a few monthly referrals and that the men could in no way have been matched to them. I typically heard something like the following comment, quoted in the news story, by a woman who said that none of the referrals had contacted her and that when she contacted them, they were not her type: "They were like retired ditch diggers."

About ten days after I signed up, I received referral slips on fourteen women, all of whom had supposedly been screened and psychologically matched to be an ideal mate for me. (Indeed, they were all markedly different from each other, and most had little in common with me.) The referral slips contained scant information limited to name, age, address, home phone, occupation, race, whether widowed or divorced, eye color, and hair color. Those I received during the first four months had also included height and weight, but this practice was later abandoned. I telephoned all my referrals to decide which ones I would meet, and in what order.

Both men and women were told by the agency that they must cooperate by calling everyone referred to them. Women found calling very difficult, partly due to tradition and values, but many tried — with unhappy results — when the calls they received from men were scant or nonexistent. The men received anywhere from eight to twenty referrals, more women than they had time to see.

Women complained that alcohol problems and lack of character were their main objections to the men they met, some using the terms "vile," "raunchy," and "vulgar." Many women also said the men were often financially strapped and that some had tried to exploit them. Moreover, they said, many of the men were extremely overweight.

I would learn, however, that the male subscribers had no monopoly on being alcoholic, impoverished, or obese. These detractions were also prevalent among the women, along with a lack of self-esteem brought about by failures in life, marital or otherwise. Their worst problems were the emotions that had prompted them, often at great financial sacrifice, to subscribe to Get A Mate — loneliness, emptiness, and fear of the future.

On the next few pages are three sets of descriptions of the

women referred to me. The first consists of notes I took while screening referrals on the telephone and includes only sketches of women I did not go on to meet. I met all the women in the second and third groups. I describe those who I thought might encounter difficulty in making a connection, and finally I describe the few I thought had a lot going for them.

NOTES FROM MY TELEPHONE SCREENING

I did not meet any of the women in this first group, but I talked to them on the phone, sometimes at length. The following are excerpts from notes I wrote on the backs of the referral slips:

Ms. A

Long telephone conversation. Sounds like a nice woman, a bit too eager to please. Lives in a mobile home and is financially strapped. Has been single for many years and seems to be looking primarily for companionship and financial support. There has been no sex in her life since her husband died, but she is "willing."

Ms. B

A forty-nine year old woman who lives in a mobile home. Seems like she is using this as a dating service rather than for marriage. Apparently likes to drink and party a lot. Somewhat opportunistic from what I could gather. Decided it would not be worthwhile to meet her.

Ms. C

She called Christmas Eve. She is an elderly born-again Christian lady, unhappy with the program. Signed up for four months. Has heard from very few referrals and was sexually propositioned by half the men who called. She says they use the service to find women for sexual purposes, that the men are not really interested in getting married. She seems very set in her ways, is unhappy living with her daughter, and plans to move back up north.

Ms. D

A little giggly, works for a bank as a clerk-typist. In poor economic circumstances, but sounds like a nice person down on her luck and fearful of the future. Mainly I felt sorry for her.

Ms. E

She called me. Another case of a woman one feels sorry for. Twice divorced, the last time from an alcoholic, she has worked hard all her life, mostly as a waitress, but most recently as a factory assembly worker. She really scraped to pay the hundreds of dollars for this dating service, and this month she got three referrals, including me. She said she subscribed as a last, desperate measure to end her loneliness. She is so desperate and needs companionship so badly that she is willing to go along with almost anything. I was kind to her — my heart went out — but I won't visit.

Ms. F

A nurse who called me. She sounded pleasant over the phone, but in the course of the long conversation I found out she is extremely overweight, weighing much more than I do. She calls this being "chunky."

Ms. G

I called and she seemed nice on the phone but is now going with someone and wants to see how that turns out before dating others. She wants to get married. Divorced fourteen years, she is afraid of growing old alone.

Ms. H

She called several times during the evening while I was out, leaving four messages on my answering machine. The first was fine, simply asking me to call back and giving her number. The other three were made in progressive stages of intoxication. Her words were slurred in the third call, and in the last she told me I was losing my big opportunity with her forever. She called again a few days later and sounded sober and civil. I told her I was dating someone else.

SOME OF THE WOMEN I MET

Having thus used the telephone to screen out many of the referrals, I arranged to meet the remaining women either at their homes or more often out for coffee and dessert. I invited a few of them out to dinner. I would learn after meeting a number of them that my telephone screening was often not very reliable.

While each of the women did have something to offer, most of them were handicapped by one or more of the following: alcoholism or alcohol dependency, marked obesity, psychological maladjustment (or were they only desperate, defeated?), and poverty. Suffering greatly and barely coping with life, the women were looking to the mating service to find men to help them hold their heads above water. If what even these women told me is true, then most of the men the service sent out possessed all of these disqualifying attributes in spades. Many of the women characterized the men as repellent, indecent slobs, exploitative and worse.

At any rate, here is a sampling of my notes on the women I met who appeared to have serious problems:

Ms. I

She is forty-eight, an unemployed office manager and nurse's aide who obviously has known better days. "Marriage happiness" is her goal according to the referral card. She was divorced twice and moved to Florida to be near her retired mother. She lives alone in a modest apartment. Her most recent divorce was caused by her husband's drinking too much and abusing her both verbally and physically. She had met him at a PWP chapter up north, and they had enjoyed "partying" a good deal.

I told her I wasn't the partying type and I was uncomfortable taking out women who liked to drink. She responded that this needn't be a problem between us, that though she liked a few drinks before dinner and especially before a date, she would be glad to have them at home alone before I picked her up. Having exhausted her savings without having found an office job here, she is now taking some schooling to become a practical nurse. She has not joined the local PWP chapter, because she is tired of singles clubs and wants to find someone to marry. She is down financially, down emotionally, and desperate. Her hopelessness and pleading only made me feel pity for her, but there was nothing I could do except treat her kindly and leave.

Ms. J

This well-educated Englishwoman has obviously known good circumstances and comes from a good family. She had married and divorced an American during World War II and later married a man she said was a bank official. After several happy years, he left her a widow, alone in America. She went back to England but found herself estranged from her family, especially her father, who was straight-laced and objected to her drinking. She rents a moderately priced condominium, but it is decorated with expensive furniture, giving credence to her claim that both her husbands had been prosperous. However, she said that both had been alcoholics.

I took her to a nice restaurant for lunch. After her fourth martini she told me that she was afraid that she herself might be developing a drinking problem, because a girlfriend had given her some literature from Alcoholics Anonymous. Her tongue loosened by the martinis, she went into some detail concerning why she was at odds with her family and her father, who was wealthy but disinheriting her. She wants to find a "good husband" and intends to quit drinking soon. She is somewhat overweight, depressed, and desperate.

With most but not all of the other women, the problem was not alcohol, though I did, from our talks about health, suspect widespread abuse of prescription drugs and occasionally illicit drugs. More often the problem was psychological maladjustment or obesity.

Ms. K

We met at a coffee shop for coffee and dessert. She is forty-eight years old and claims to have been married to an alcoholic. She blamed him for having caused her to become a foodaholic, but amazingly doesn't seem to realize how obese she actually is. Over the extremely rich dessert she ordered, she said it would be nice if she could lose six pounds or so. Sixty would be more like it. She is what I have begun to think of as a "professional parent," a person excessively tied to and dependent on his or her adult children. She talks about her daughter and son-in-law all the time. She lives with them because they need her financial support, and they are having a rough time emotionally as well. She makes a good living selling real estate, but she gives the impression of being money-hungry. She is looking for someone to marry and expects to be fully supported by her new husband, wanting to leave her daughter as well off as possible. Her entire life and reason for being seems to revolve around her daughter, who is "the only one I have in the world."

One runs into all kinds of people in a mating service. Some are good, solid, and hard-working but nevertheless handicapped by the circumstances of their upbringing or past marriages. Their lives have been hard, they have known deprivation, and they sometimes suffer from lack of self-esteem and repeatedly allow themselves to be exploited.

Ms. L

She was born into an impoverished rural family and given little education. Even so, she is an agreeable person and a hard worker. She has a history of being repeatedly exploited — first by her family, then by a husband, and later by a succession of men friends. She worked her way up to being a factory foreman and on a small income raised three children, the youngest being seventeen and still living at home. Her house is modest, but clean and uncluttered. She does not especially like her job and hopes to get some schooling to become a nurse after her youngest child leaves home. In all ways she is well-meaning, a good salt-of-the-earth type of person, but far too eager to please and be liked. At 5'8" and 123 pounds, she is quite thin. She was born a farmer's daughter and married young to "get away from home." She feels that she was happy in her marriage for fifteen years until her husband "went berserk" and abandoned the family. She then married and supported a fundamentalist country preacher. He was stern, strict, and "everything that was fun was a sin." She divorced him but lost out financially.

She looks worn out, much older than her forty-one years. Her luck with men continues to be bad. Most recently, she was cut adrift after going steady for three years with a divorced man she had known from childhood, after having paid all their joint dating expenses because he was always broke. When his financial position finally did improve, he left her and took up with another woman. She was down and desperately lonely, and I felt terribly sorry for her.

Most of the women were under financial pressure, but not all of them. A small minority were actually rich.

Ms. M

The referral slip said she was in her early forties and gave really good numbers for height and weight. However, there was a "retired" notation under "occupation" which made me wonder. The card also said she was a "beautiful lady," and this turned out to be fact, not fiction. (I had seen similar notations before for many ladies, but the fact had little resemblance to the description.) I later learned that she had come from an affluent family, had gone to good schools, and had briefly attended a good college.

When I arranged for a dinner date on the phone, she said she would send me a map showing how to get to her house. The directions came on expensive stationery, tastefully displaying her initials. The note read: "Hope this map will get you to my house. You sound *awfully intelligent*. I'll start through my Funk & Wagnall's again! Give me a break — I only had one year of college. P.S. (She drew an arrow to the word 'Funk.') No, that's not a dirty word!"

Her house is good-sized and located in a good, settled, middle-class neighborhood, but it is sorely neglected and looks run-down — in fact, it is somewhat of an eyesore in the neighborhood. Especially noticeable is the overgrown shrubbery around her windows and front door. The police once recommended that she cut the shrubs back because they invite burglars, but she refused because she likes the privacy.

When she opened the door to greet me, my first thought was that she looked like a slightly-faded Vivien Leigh, with the same pretty face and great figure. My second thought was that the inside of the house looked like a mess! Uncharitably, I thought it must have been housework that she had retired from.

Driving to the restaurant for dinner, her conversation was unusual and most interesting. She said she had just broken up with a gentleman she had been living with. He was retired, prosperous, and had taken her to many fine restaurants and on some exciting weekend trips. Initially, she avoided telling me anything about her background and sidestepped all serious questions by taking off on humorous tangents. She is very intelligent, lots of fun, and completely uninhibited.

After dinner she invited me back to her house to talk and listen to some records. Soon after we had put on some music and settled down on her sofa, she got up and said she wanted to change in to something more comfortable. When she re-emerged from her bedroom she was wearing a sexy negligee, like something from Frederick's of Hollywood. I thought, This kind of thing can only happen in the movies — or maybe to some lucky woman-charmer, not to an ordinary fellow like me. Then I thought, What do I do now? I remember worrying about the V.D. risk among promiscuous people.

Only once before had I experienced anything like this. I met a lady through one of the singles clubs, where she enjoyed a good reputation. She was an amateur belly dancer and as we entered a months-long relationship she agreed to give me a private exhibition one night in her living room. She changed into an exotic costume, put a belly-dancing tape on her stereo, and proceeded to show me what she could do — which was plenty! But back to Ms. M:

She came from a wealthy family and married a childhood friend, also a privileged person. He was initially successful in business, and their marriage had gone well for a decade or so, but he (and she) had gradually become addicted to and debilitated by alcohol and drugs. He eventually died relatively young from diseases of the liver and pancreas, and she started dating younger men. She liked the ambience and lifestyle she found among rock musicians, and for a while she traveled from city to city with a rock group, using marijuana and cocaine. She eventually became extremely ill, came back to her empty house, and with the help of family obtained medical attention and improved somewhat, though her doctor still finds it necessary to maintain her on psychotropic drugs, possibly explaining her mood swings, phobias, and occasional bizarre behavior.

Like all the other women clients, she was critical of Get A Mate, though she apparently used the service frequently. It was she who gave me the clipping of the newspaper exposé on Nicholson with the notation "When I get fleeced, I get fleeced!" I soon realized how ill this lovely woman was, and I was relieved when I got a call telling me goodbye, that she had found a boyfriend.

Ms. N

The widow of a successful businessman and most of a day's drive away, she is a wealthy woman living in a large, lavishly furnished home, complete with swimming pool, located in an exclusive beach community. She is extremely health conscious, and her daily swimming provides her with a splendid figure for a woman of forty-nine. That is the good news; all the rest is bad. She seems so strange that it is uncomfortable talking to her, and she is extremely fearful of just about everything, particularly old age and death — she constantly talks about both.

Her husband's business kept him out of town most of the time, so to fill the hours she did volunteer work in a nursing home for a few hours a week. Now she works there full-time as a salaried employee, though she obviously doesn't need the money. I believed her when she said she had been left a six-figure income.

She says she is unhappy and isolated from her friends and family, especially her only child, who went away to college. She likes mostly to talk about the nursing home and its inhabitants, whose past accomplishments are in some cases noteworthy and whose present deterioration, which she describes in detail, discomforting. A health and religious fanatic, she sins not at all — no drinking, smoking, gambling, or sex.

I felt sorry for this neurotic rich lady and found myself hoping that she would indeed find Heaven after her death — because her life appeared to be Hell.

Some women were still emotionally devastated from a recent death or divorce, but they definitely had the potential to make someone a good wife — maybe as many as twenty percent of them. They needed time to recover from their traumas, but instead of gathering the courage to get out and meet people in Real World activities or in Single World, they took what they thought would be the easy way out and subscribed to Get A Mate, falling unawares into Casual World.

The following thumbnail sketches describe some of the women I met who had a good deal to offer the right man. Some still needed to work through their emotional turmoil of divorce; others, divorced and socially active for some time, erroneously felt that they were too old at forty or fifty to have men in their lives or to build new social lives.

Based on their experiences in Get A Mate, they lamented that there were simply fewer eligible men than women, that the good men were either taken or didn't need Get A Mate, that only the sick, the mentally and physically lame, and the impoverished did.

Ms. O

Now in her fifties, in her professional prime she was a well-known figure in one of the performing arts. She lives in a nice house in a good neighborhood, but she is in the midst of divorce proceedings that keep her in an extremely emotional state. A nice-looking woman still working part-time at her art, she is nevertheless at loose ends because her social life and male companionship have all but disappeared. It was at her daughter's urging that she subscribed to the Get A Mate service. In spite of her quick intelligence, cosmopolitan outlook, and education, she feels that at her age it would be difficult to find a man she could enjoy life with and maybe settle down with again. She is obviously a doer and a survivor, and I know she will be okay.

I did not date her again, because she was involved in the divorce proceedings. I later learned she had joined some of the groups I had suggested, had a boyfriend, and was moving along nicely on the road to emotional recovery.

Ms. P

Physically trim, and at forty-eight a middle-level executive for a medium-sized corporation, she indicated on her referral card that her interests were swimming, dining, theater, bridge, golf, and tennis. I decided to take her to dinner at a French restaurant. Her home, located in a nice neighborhood in a good part of town, is beautifully furnished and nicely kept up. She is bright — a sharp, down-to-earth, no-nonsense lady — but has an unsmiling, too-serious personality. (She alone, of all the women I met through Get A Mate, had negotiated a cheaper fee.)

She had been married to a noncommissioned officer who retired and took to drink and deteriorated, and they were divorced. She took a job as a secretary of a new firm, and her alert intelligence, willingness to work, and take-charge personality quickly secured her a responsible, well-paying position. But with all of her expertise and bottom-line business skills, she has allowed herself to become an isolated workaholic, lonely and unhappy.

Holding her back more than the job is the fact that she feels she is "over the hill" in her late forties as far as men are concerned. But boredom and hating to come home to an empty house after work finally prompted her to seek help from Get A Mate. Her first referral was a "live one." However, he had been just recently divorced, and obsessed with remarrying as soon as possible, he proposed to her the very first night they met. She wonders if she should have accepted. She complained about the suitability of the men referred to her, and I encouraged her to try some of the singles clubs and travel clubs, assuring her that she was not too old to do so.

I later saw her at some PWP socials and once on a singles cruise; she was apparently having a good time. Though I later lost track of her, she is a nice lady and I think she is going to make a happy adjustment.

Ms. Q

I met her for lunch at a family restaurant. A highly educated, intelligent, and pleasant woman, she is a retired college professor still teaching part-time. At sixty-one, she is alert, good company, and a good conversationalist. She is comfortably situated in a nice mobile home park. She is cheerful and outgoing, and she keeps herself busy. Except for a degree of loneliness, she is a fairly happy and well-adjusted person. She has a number of friends and friendly acquaintances but nevertheless wants a man to share her life with, and thus she subscribed to Get A Mate. Because of the kind of men the service sends out, however, she is thankful that they are so few in number.

I am relatively certain that by now she has made a good adjustment to life as a single person. Possibly she is married. I don't know. I do know she is a nice person with a lot to recommend her.

Ms. R

A salt-of-the-earth type and a fine, decent woman, she lives in good middle-class circumstances in an upscale mobile home park. She is considerate, pleasant to talk to, and extremely religious. Now retired from her job as a school teacher, she is careful of her health and diet-conscious, and she exercises regularly. She is good-looking and trim for a woman in her fifties. A fundamentalist Christian, she has been on pilgrimages to the Holy Land. She wants to remarry but is aghast at the referrals the agency has been sending her.

I recall thinking as I drove home from lunch with her that she would be a splendid match for someone who shared her religious beliefs.

Ms. S

This Frenchwoman enjoyed a cosmopolitan, jet-set lifestyle prior to the death of her husband, whom she had met and married during World War II. He had become quite wealthy, his money working for him in various glamorous European capitals, and when he died a decade ago he left her the resources to live very well. Even though she lost some of her money in bad investments, she can still afford to live in a luxurious oceanfront condominium and own a summer cottage on an island in the Mediterranean.

At fifty-nine, she is now lonely and unhappy and feels left out from the "two-by-two" social world she used to enjoy. She has an exceptional figure and keeps in shape by playing tennis, swimming daily, and watching her diet. She likes to be seen at fancy French restaurants, where she actually eats very little, and enjoys the theater, art, and travel. She maintains a small library with one shelf sporting a good collection of erotica. She is classy, uninhibited, sensual, and slightly aggressive in a clever and cajoling but charming way.

Though she is somewhat opinionated, she has an excellent sense of humor. There's no question she would make the right man an excellent spouse, but she is experiencing great difficulty finding Mr. Reasonably Right — someone with the means and background to fit into her cosmopolitan and elegant lifestyle. The few available eligibles in her social circle and, she laughs, "those about to become eligible," are fiercely competed for by her peers and too often opt for younger women.

Feeling she had nothing to lose, she tried Get A Mate but is appalled by the men the agency is sending her despite its assurances that they would send her classy men. She considered a lawsuit but decided against it after complaining to the agency.

I dated her for a while, but she was really out of my league financially and socially, so after I received the following note from her, I offered to put her in touch with a fellow in the Adventure Travel Club who had a nice boat: "Well, after three months of cruising the Mediterranean, I know I can only be happy in close contact with the sea. So, after our brief encounter, do you mind introducing me to your friend? After all, we could contribute to your last chapter."

I should emphasize here that these last three women were, each in her own way, exceptional. I had been referred to over one hundred women by Get A Mate, actually meeting fewer than half of them after my telephone screening. Of the ones I did meet, fewer than half struck me as having something solid to offer to a potential Mr. Reasonably Right. The overall statistics point to the probability that about twenty percent were good prospects but were having difficulty because the available pool of men in their forties, fifties, and sixties was small. One hundred percent of the women were critical of the men referred to them.

A better and more economical approach if you are bound and determined to try Casual World would be to tailor a personal ad and place it in the classified section of your hometown newspaper (if they accept them) or in a singles magazine or special-interest magazine. Or you could subscribe to an inexpensive dating service where they do not interview you at home but allow you to apply by phone or at their office and pay a *small* fee to put you in touch with people who may be suitable — and making no promises, implied or otherwise, to find you a mate.

Either way, you still face the risks encountered in meeting strangers, so it is up to you to screen people, first by phone and then in a public place from which you can conveniently and politely leave if necessary. How effective this approach is as a means of finding a mate can only be guessed at, because people will almost never admit to friends or family that they found a spouse, a relate, or even a date through a dating service or personal ad. Whether or not you opt to place a personal ad, the next chapter will familiarize you with this frequently utilized corner of Casual World.

12.

Mr. (Ms.) Wonderful, That's Me!

The headline over a feature article in the *St. Petersburg Times* reads: "Personal Ads Seeking Romance Now Reach into Middle America." The newspaper itself still refuses to accept ads of this type, however, because they feel it takes too much manpower "to police these things." On the other hand, many other legitimate newspapers and magazines do accept such ads, and an increasing number of ordinary people are using them.

DO CLASSIFIED ADS WORK?

Do they really work? Apparently some do work some of the time, and they certainly work better than most other Casual World approaches. As with the dating services, few people are inclined to admit that they rely on advertising to find dates, and couples almost always say they met each other through a friend or because of a shared interest in Real World or, to a lesser extent, Single World. One local singles magazine carried a standing offer to pay for the marriage licenses of couples who met through its classified ads, and though they didn't publish any positive results during the relatively brief existence of the periodical, they might very well have succeeded in bringing some couples to the altar. If so, the people involved opted against saving the few dollars the license cost by making public their manner of meeting.

Almost always those matches that do take place go unheralded. However, an informative article by Jennifer Lowe in the *Los Angeles Daily News* in September 1987 showed that where there is burning desire, there is sometimes hope. Lowe cited three examples where the ads were successful in making matches, two failures, and one (probably from among thousands) in which fun and games were sought and found.

Lowe tells about the good fortune of one woman who met and married a "forty-one-year-old Los Angeles County probation department supervisor who loves Woody Allen movies, doesn't hate his mother, and isn't fascinated with Hitler — just as her ad specified." A public relations consultant was also successful. She advertised for "a special, well-educated man unafraid to show his feelings, healthy and open to the unexpected, with interests in sunsets, playgrounds, and Barry Manilow." She married an accountant who answered her ad — the first personal ad he had ever answered. In another example, a woman's ad caused sudden lightning to strike: "When we got there it was like two magnets crossing the room. By the time we got to the elevator, we were hooked."

Lowe's research showed that whereas personal ads were once thought of solely as *modi operandi* for the lovelorn, that has all changed:

> Now personal ads are the "trend of the times," said Vicki Youngman, a *Los Angeles Daily News* classified advertising manager. The *Daily News* has begun a classified column called Encounters, similar to a new personals column in the *Los Angeles Times*. *California Business* started its classified column, Executive Introductions, earlier this year. *Los Angeles* magazine carries a popularly read section called Matchmaker, Matchmaker.

Us magazine, which puts the number of publications running personals nationwide at 500, estimates that 2 million people run personal ads every year, and more than 10 million answer them. Of those numbers, 10,000 meet and get married.

The ads' popularity might be because of something that has caused singles to rethink their strategies of late: AIDS.

"If you meet a guy or girl in a bar, you're not going to go up and ask on the first encounter if they've had sex in the last ten years," said Vi Rogers, editor of the Norwalk-based *National Singles Register*. "But through a personal ad, when a person calls or they're writing back and forth, they can be really open."

Others attribute the upswing in personals to changing times.

"It's an acceptable way to meet respectable people — it's become more mainstream," said Liz Hargrove, a Los Angeles marriage and family counselor who has run a singles group for a decade.

That's the good news. The bad news is that many ads either grossly exaggerate the writers' qualifications or are deceptive. As one woman in the article put it, "'Cute and cuddly' could be a three-hundred-pound, overweight blob." Accordingly, ads often lead to disillusionment: "A forty-four year old Hollywood screenwriter met a man who described himself as the most exciting man in town. He kept falling asleep." Another example in Lowe's article was: "A seventy year old Glendale resident answered an ad hoping to meet a college graduate with blond hair. Instead he was met by an eighty year old woman wearing a full-length black satin dress and gold tiara."

Very frequently — probably for the most part — classified ads are simply intended to invite people to come out and play. One man in Lowe's article ran a full-page ad in which he opened, "Are you more than just a pretty face? Generous, creative businessman wants to find a hot, sexy woman with a good sense of humor." That forty-nine year old marketing consultant met his thirty-five year old match, and "the two have been dating and working together since." Neither, however, would recommend the ad technique to find a Mr. or Ms. Reasonably Right. Maybe they know something from their previous experiences that most of the rest of us don't.

The classified ads definitely do offer advantages over the competing corners of Casual World. An ad can be directly aimed at a target group you're interested in and written to appeal only to certain specific types of people. "Middle-aged lady seeking middle-aged man interested in dancing and classical music" will get one kind of response; "Sweet young thing looking for rich male who likes things sweet and young" will bring forth quite another.

SCREENING "APPLICANTS"

Classified ads are a do-it-yourself project. You write the ads, you place them, and you screen the responses. A big advantage over the singles bars is that you are not under the influence of alcohol or under pressure to find a date by closing time, so it's easy to say no when someone doesn't seem suitable. Besides, you usually have plenty of "applicants" to choose from.

Advertising does have some of the drawbacks inherent in all Casual World encounters, however. It means lots of trial-and-error screening because it's impossible to tell with any certainty over the phone whether some contacts will turn out to be a waste of time. Moreover, as anywhere else in Casual World (or Single World or Real World), there are always risks. However, it has often been said that to live is to take risks, that risks are involved in everything we do. In this instance we try to minimize them by improving screening skills. Like other social abilities, such skills are partly intuitive and partly gained by practice.

MINIMIZING RISKS

If you decide to try the ads, follow the caveats that were given in the dating service chapter about meeting people. Have the respondents telephone you or write to you in care of a box number at the periodical or at the post office. Don't thoughtlessly give out your address to someone. Meet for the first time in a public place where you can politely leave if anything about the person bothers or frightens you. A final bit of advice: While Casual World can provide easy dating opportunities, it does not offer a supporting social network of friends and acquaintances, and there may be periods of isolation between your one-on-one dating trysts. If you do go this route for a while, be sure to maintain ties in Real World and Single World. It's nice to have friends and a home base to return to.

WRITING AND PLACING ADS

Where should you place your ad? Ads in the local media may be the most productive, because the people who respond will live nearby, facilitating your meeting them and subsequent dating if a relationship develops. The other option is to advertise in one of the nationally circulated periodicals which carry such ads, but you may find that geography can become an obstacle for Cupid's arrows.

Letters are nice, but the person usually turns out to be quite different from the one you read into the letters you received. A natural tendency is to endow a pen pal with all the attributes of an ideal mate. Exchanging photographs helps, as do telephone conversations, but there's no substitute for frequent face-to-face encounters.

Tailor your ad to target the specific types of people you want to meet. One woman to whom religion was a key factor in life wisely advertised in a magazine directed to people who are similarly inclined. Her ad in *Solo* told prospective suitors exactly what she was and was not interested in:

> POETESS. Petite widow seeks non-carnal Christian highly educated 55 up. Spirit-filled man of God, practicing God's presence in work, prayer, play. Emotionally, financially secure. Sense of humor!

Sophisticated people and intellectuals might look for their counterparts by advertising in periodicals like *The New York Review of Books*. The following accurately conveyed in a few words the kind of man the writer was looking for and the kind of woman she thought herself to be:

> Little, brainy, and beautiful seeks licit liaison. Pianist/ scholar, pedigreed, friendly, proud, whimsical DJF [Divorced Jewish Female] hankers after corrigible male, 45-55 with large heart, true-grit, accomplishment. Prefer genius.

Personal ads found in local or regional slick magazines sometimes have a poetic twist. In the Tampa-St. Petersburg area, *Singles Life* magazine carried the following:

> If you like to eat, I like to cook. If you like to read, I've got the book. Talkative, happy, and play racquetball well, These are the things that ring my bell. Need male 40 or more who knows his own mind, With good moral standards, gentle and kind. And so I will end my personal ad. Your quick response may make us both glad.

The woman who had inserted the above ad was blond, forty-five, and tastefully dressed. She looked a bit like Liv Ullmann. Divorced for fifteen years, she had held back on dating while raising her three children. Now that her last child had left home, she wanted to enjoy a more active social life and meet some men. Not knowing what to say about herself that would "make someone want to meet me and still be honest," she turned to a friend to compose the ad. It drew twelve responses, and she decided to meet three of the men. She dated one of them for several months until he moved out of town, and then she placed another ad.

Here's another, from a man who called himself a veteran ad writer. He averaged about four responses from each and considered personal ads to be his primary method of meeting women, much preferred to cruising the bars.

> I don't own a yacht and my hobbies don't include collecting antique sports cars. I don't even own a Learjet so my travels don't include jetting to Paris for lunch. There's some pretty stiff competition on this page, but if you're looking for an honest, fun-loving and witty guy, 30, 5'10", trim, with a good job and interesting lifestyle, then drop me a note telling me you're slender, childless, and looking for a close, long-lasting relationship with someone who will return your affection, caring, love, and laughter.

This experienced public relations man claimed to be a bit cautious, and perhaps he was a bit cynical as well. He had a firm requirement that all his dates be childless because "I've met women with four or five kids whose rigid requirements for a man are two legs and breathing. They just want someone to feed the kids and pay the rent."

A woman to whom thirty meant any age from thirty to thirty-nine had forty-five responses to her ad. That her real age was thirty-eight shows that there is a certain amount of on-going hoaxing. Those playing the casual dating game should expect it.

> Versatile, vivacious, and attractive. Enjoys sports, all music, theater, dancing, dining, and quiet times. I'm a feminine 5'4" with auburn hair, green eyes, and I enjoy being 30. Would like to know how you enjoy life.

THE CORNUCOPIA

Individuals who are skillful in composing personal ads find that where they may once have had difficulty in finding dates, they now suddenly encounter a veritable horn of plenty. A female professor described herself so effectively that her ad drew nearly fifty responses. Of all the men she met at the time, or through subsequent ads, there was only one she felt she should have married. "I liked him and he liked me a lot," she said, but at the time she wasn't looking for a serious relationship. She later regretted letting her single golden opportunity slip by.

That can happen to anyone suddenly presented with an over-abundance of dates. You never know if someone in the next batch of responses will be "better." But to quote one woman, "That's what I like about the ads. Unlike being at a cocktail party or a bar, I don't have to fall in love with the person sitting next to me because he's there. I can be infinitely more selective right in the privacy of my home." Getting dates this way can be compared to shopping in a Sears catalog: you pick out what you think you want, and if it doesn't satisfy you, there's unlimited free exchange — and new products coming onto the market all the time.

ONE MAN'S EXPERIENCES

Remember my old friend Mr. Friendly, who had investigated the New York dating services for me? At my behest he also did some research on personal ads and reported back as follows:

> Okay, now we get to another interesting aspect of the dating business. As I told you — or as you told me — another way to meet people is to put an ad in the singles magazines or newspapers. That's what I did. It's a rather sophisticated publication, and interesting overall. They list the activities available for singles, for example, raps and

socials, self-help groups, cocktail parties, concerts, workshops, gallery talks, duplicate bridge, lectures, videotapes, foreign film series, chess, and mix-and-match tennis. It's a nice magazine to have around.

They also have classified personals. As opposed to some publications, you don't see any weird ones. Here are a couple of examples:

> Single white Catholic male, 59, lawyer, gardening, classical music, travel, tennis.

> Affluent, handsome, divorced male executive, currently lives aboard a sailing yacht in Stanford in the summers and in New Rochelle in the winters. Desires adventurous and affectionate, slender gal as companion for summer sailing and winter skiing weekends. Humorous, spontaneous, and athletic. 44, 5'10", 175.

Okay, now I'll give you the ad I placed:

> Single white male, 6 ft., 185, handsome, well-educated professional, would like to meet attractive, warm, sincere, loving, classy, single white female who enjoys dining, dancing, theater, music, and quiet moments together. Please send photo and phone number.

There's also a box number, which is nice because it gives you total anonymity. The letters are delivered to the magazine; then those addressed to me are mailed to me in a large envelope. I ran the ad in January, February, and March, which turned out to be too long. I received over fifty responses in three months. Of the fifty, I dated fifteen. Again, overall it was an excellent experience. I met some very nice people, good looking, well situated, well paid — women pretty much on their way up. I think the key word I used in the ad was "classy." A lot of women like to think of themselves as being classy, and for the most part they were.

Here is one response that came in:

> I am also going it alone. 5'5", 115 lbs., blond hair and blue eyes. Gemini people love to talk with others who enjoy life. I am an avid reader and very interested in music. I don't smoke, enjoy wine in moderation.

I went out with her and she was physically a very attractive woman. She did have some emotional problems which she hadn't resolved. Her husband had passed away, and one moment she was cheerful, and the next, sad.

I also went out with an artist. I really liked her. A super person.

Very attractive. We dated a couple of times. She's probably a few years older than me; she never would tell me her age. Anyway, here's what her response to my ad looked like:

> Couldn't resist. I'm blond, long hair, very attractive, sense of humor, sense of the absurd, over-educated, successful professional. Let's meet. Sounds adventurous.

Here's another response:

> Allow me to introduce myself. I am attractive, sincere, warm, classy, and elegant. Like to dance, dine, go to the theater. Love music, and I especially like a quiet time together with a man I care about. I am also a well-educated professional. You sound amazingly good! You sound very direct, bright, handsome. Looks count for me, too, I must admit. I think I'm really pretty. And quiet moments with a person you are attracted to can really be quite nice. I'll tell you some of the things I do: I go to school, I'm a singer, thirty-one, and I like comedy in addition to what you mentioned. I like the French language and travel, and I like men as friends better than women. I like TV and movies better than books — totally unchic, I know. I like a million things. I'd like to speak on the phone with you so we can get a sense of each other.

I also went out with a teacher who responded to my ad. She was a nice lady, and I really did enjoy her company. We went out and had lunch one day and then for an evening, a week or two later, to a movie and then back to her place afterwards.

I often intend to see a woman again, but I have so many responses to check out I never get back to them. It gets to be too much, and I can't afford to take all the women out so much. I just become tired. I think one week I saw five different women.

Anyway, I'm sitting here with about thirty-five more responses, and I haven't talked to one of these women. There are some that I just absolutely would not go out with because of the way the letter is written. One I won't bother to respond to wrote:

> Let's get together. I'm big and beautiful, 5'6" and 215 pounds...

The letters I was most likely to respond to came from women who sounded positive, really interested, and ready to get together. The stationery they used didn't necessarily matter. Some were on notebook paper, others on nice letter paper. It's the content that mattered. I think it's better without a photograph; that way there is always the element of surprise, the element of curiosity. Summing up, I would say that advertising in a slick singles magazine has to be the best way yet to meet a lot of people. One aspect, though, is that most of us, including me, don't want to admit we use advertisements to get dates. I told a few close friends, but I'm not about to tell just anyone I know. I really don't feel I'm the type of guy who really has to find dates this way. But in the 1980's I don't think there is time for a lot of single people, especially young professionals, to go to the bars to meet people. I've been in the New York City area for about two and a half years now. I'm busy, and I travel a lot. I don't have a chance to meet many women around here.

One of the pluses of using the ads is that you can screen everyone at your leisure, and you can call when you have the time. Occasionally I would call someone and go out with her that same Saturday night. Once it was Sunday and I wasn't doing anything, so I called a woman. It was about six o'clock. We talked for awhile and got along pretty well. Finally I said, "Hell, I'll be over in about an hour." That was okay with her, so we went out and got something to eat. I never took her out again, but she was nice.

Overall, I like this method of finding dates. I did remember your request to ask women who placed ads what they thought about the results they were getting. The consensus was that they were not really happy with the dates they got from advertising. Not like I was, anyway. Maybe most of the guys who write these ads or answer them tend to be losers. Most of the gals said they met some interesting men from time to time, but no bells rang with any of their dates.

Many kinds of publications take singles ads, but you have to be careful. There are publications like the *Village Voice*, which will print *anything*. Other publications aim at the intellectuals and business people, and then there are the slick singles magazines, like the one Mr. Friendly used, which flourish in most metropolitan areas. The cost of placing a personal ad compares to the cost of a dinner date, and the ads offer as good a return on investment, measured in numbers of responses, as any technique in Casual World.

BACK TO REALITY

What about those who are primarily looking for caring, committed relationships? When it comes to sharing interests, sharing friends, and getting to know someone well enough to fall in love, Real World is your best bet, with the Single World of clubs and travel a close second. I noticed that those who involved themselves in Casual World often developed tendencies to isolate themselves from support groups and not to take any particular dates very seriously. Casual World, which so many people enter in hopes of finding security and permanence, is in fact a superficial milieu characterized by a transient lifestyle. After a while, I found the whole exercise of meeting strangers in Casual World boring. Apparently, so did my friend who researched the scene in New York City. He summed up his experiences as follows:

> I would like to give a word of caution about this whole business of meeting the opposite sex through dating services and personal ads. It's all very interesting, but it can be awfully confusing and risky. Sometimes you find the real gems right in your own backyard. Maybe what I'm finally learning is to take the time to get to know a person. It would be far more to my benefit than trying to date so many women. I'm going to try to take an interest in one person for a while and see what happens. If we get along on the first date, I'll try a second and then a third instead of jumping around so much.
>
> On the other hand, I might just remain single. Maybe I'll never get married, but I'd hate to think that down the line, when I get older, I would have to live my life all alone. I really mean that. I've had a lot of wonderful experiences I would never have been able to enjoy had I been married, but I can't stay back in time. Maybe they were okay for then, but I have to go forward.
>
> What bothers me, though, is that a lot of my friends say how fortunate I am to be single. Many people I know are either close to divorce or are divorced — sometimes even twice. But then I suppose life is one big risk. So that's what I'm going to change. I think meeting you and having a chance to go over some of these options has been really enlightening. I've really enjoyed doing this research and hope it's helpful to you and to those who read your book.

WHEN RELATIONSHIPS BECOME SERIOUS

About the time my friend (now married) was considering changing his lifestyle by finding someone with whom to enter into a lasting relationship, I was beset with the same yearning for involvement with one special person and decided to change my lifestyle. Remember the woman from the Single World circles I regularly ran with, the one who had been an acquaintance for a year or two and whom I frequently bumped into at singles club activities like the weekly bridge game — Miss Tagalong, with whom I had toured the museums during the Mexico City vacation described in the travel chapter? We entered into a close and caring relationship for a four year period.

This brings us to the subject of the next chapter, the various ways that mature middle-agers construct a framework for committed relationships. Remarriage used to be the only option, but now several alternatives have emerged.

13.

Love and Marriage

Over the course of a lifetime, most people fall in love more than once, and they love different people in different ways and with different intensities. Love *is* "a many-splendored thing," a highly individual thing — and a most complex and powerful one!

In past years when a couple discovered they were in love, or were "struck by" or "fell into" love, a union usually occurred which was both legally and religiously sanctioned — that is, they got married. Today, alternative arrangements such as "living together" are common. Also, because of circumstances, many other couples opt for just "going steady" or "going together," that is, living separately but remaining in an exclusive relationship in which the couple see each other frequently, perhaps daily; depend on each other to meet many of their needs, such as emotional succor and sexual gratification; and assist each other with the daily problems of living. Other couples enter into "in God's Eye" marriages, sanctioned by a clergyman but not by the state.

Each of these remating arrangements has its advantages and disadvantages and needs to be looked at in the context of the changing relationship of the sexes in American society, but let's begin by reviewing some contemporary thinking on the phenomenon we call "love." After all, everything begins with love.

WHAT IS THIS THING CALLED LOVE?

The phenomenon of love in its various manifestations, like religious faith, does not easily lend itself to description. Like faith, love is experienced differently by different people and even differently by the same person at different times in his or her life. Much has been written about love, as we well know.

One scholar investigating the phenomenon, Dr. John Alan Lee, based the research for his book Colours of Love on hundreds of references to love in Western literature ranging from Plato and the Bible to modern novels. Eventually he categorized his findings into six hypothetical styles of love: eros (love of beauty), storge (compassionate love), ludus (playful love), mania (obsessive love), agape (altruistic love), and pragma (realistic love).

Eros, according to Lee's summary of his research in *Psychology Today*, involves an immediate, powerful attraction to the physical appearance of the beloved. "Erotic lovers typically felt a chemical or gut reaction on meeting each other; heightened heartbeat is not just a figment of fiction, it seems, but the erotic lover's physiological response to meeting the dream." Lee holds that while modern usage equates the erotic with the sexual, eros involves much more. "Erotic lovers actively and imaginatively cultivate many sexual techniques to preserve the delight in the partner's body," but they also seek "a deep rapport with their beloved." Because erotic lovers place so much emphasis on physical attraction, however, they are often disappointed. Lee found that the purer the erotic qualities of love in a relationship, the less the chances of developing a mutual, lasting union.

Storge (pronounced stor-gay), or compassionate love, in contrast to eros, builds slowly over time to become "a peaceful and enchanting affection, without fever, tumult, or folly." Lee says that storgic love sneaks up unnoticed, that "storgic lovers remember no special point when they fell in love." Sex usually occurs late in this kind of relationship, developing naturally "with the passage of time and the enjoyment of shared activities." In essence, "you grow accustomed to her face."

Ludus, as described by Lee, comes from the Roman poet Ovid's term *amor ludens*, playful love, love as a game. The ludic lover does not become too attached or intimate and typically has more than one partner at the same time. We see a lot of this, of course, in Casual World.

Mania (obsessive love) is characterized by heartache, sleeplessness, loss of appetite, and similar symptoms. "The manic lover is consumed by thoughts of the beloved," alternating between ecstasy and despair, and he or she is possessive and jealous to an extreme.

Agape (pronounced ah-ga-pay) is patient, sacrificing, altruistic love. All the great religions share this ideal in their teachings.

Last but not least is pragma (realistic love), often characteristic of mature middle-agers, but by no means limited to them. "The pragmatic approach to love argues that lovers should choose each other on the basis of compatible personalities, like interests and education, similar backgrounds and religious views, and the like," says Lee. "The pragmatic lover uses social activities as a means to an end and will drop them if there is no payoff in partners."

Needless to say, few of us have experienced love only according to one of these styles. Our styles often change as we progress through life, we love different partners with different styles, and we usually love a person in more than one of these ways.

A related book on the subject is *A New Look at Love* by Elaine and G. William Walston. They use the term "passionate love" to describe a phenomenon similar Lee's eros, and "compassionate love" parallels storge. The authors invite the reader to decide which love is preferable: "The electric, tingly excitement, almost unbearable in intensity, that makes being near a lover almost as urgent as getting your next breath of air? Or the gentle warmth and comfort of a mate who will share our pleasures, griefs, and triumphs not only today, but ten years from now?" Most people want both, and many of us do experience both, often sequentially rather than concurrently: the one in our youth, the other later on.

The Walstons point out that passionate love tends to be relatively short-lived because it is difficult or impossible to enjoy the thrill of its red-hot exciting nature while simultaneously basking in the warm glow of a quiet, secure, and deepening companionate relationship. While passionate love can readily be spent, companionate love can last through a lifetime. The authors observe that there are no easy answers to questions concerning the two, no universal solutions: "There is no tried and true recipe for mixing just the right amount of passionate and companionate love into your marriage. People change, their personalities change, their bodies change. As they change, their desires change."

People who tend to be romantics may find it depressing that other researchers concur in the observation that the longer a couple remains together, the less passionately they tend to love each other. Nor are most romantics comfortable with the assertion that sex and love can be separated. But they can be. Eric Fromm, for one, asserts that "sexual desire can easily blend with and be stimulated by any strong emotion, of which love is only one." In his book *The Art of Loving*, he points out that even from infancy men and women often respond to disturbing events with a sexual response and, furthermore, that sexual desire "can be stimulated by the anxiety of loneliness, by the wish to conquer or be conquered, by vanity, by the wish to hurt and even destroy, as much as by love."

To be sure, most of these concepts and descriptions of love are not news to middle-agers. Sometimes, though, as we rush headlong into a relationship, we lose sight of all we have learned about love over the years. This is okay — in fact, better than okay and often wonderful — but unfortunately, as with anything pleasurable, there are pitfalls.

LOVE AND SEX

Lucy Taylor, in a perceptive article in *Single* magazine, observed: "Adrenaline, then, makes the heart grow fonder. Fear and frustration can fuel passionate love, a fact substantiated by love affairs beset by obstacles. Nothing seals the bond of an adolescent romance more firmly than the parents who attempt to break it up. Wartime romances, extramarital affairs, and unrequited passion are all intensified by the very dangers and difficulties lovers face in just getting together."

Ann Landers put it more succinctly for "Crushed in Connecticut," who wrote in and asked, "Is it possible to be in love with one person and engage in sex with another?" Ann's answer: "Sometimes sex has very little to do with love. It can be the result of too much Scotch, an accumulation of hostility or anger toward a loved one, sheer biological need due to separation, seduction by a smoothie, vulnerability related to insecurity, or a loss of self-esteem."

All this brings to mind the preoccupation of many people with such questions as: What is true love? How can you tell whether it's love or infatuation? Is time the true test of love, or can people be in love even if they know they will be together only briefly, never to see each other again? Is love a kind of temporary insanity? Can love be harmful? Can it even kill? What is love sickness?

Mary Wack, a Stanford researcher who studied the phenomenon of "love sickness" as chronicled during the Middle Ages, found that both medieval literature and medical writings gave serious consideration to the problem, which they believed to be a genuine physical malady. Interestingly, separate "cures" were prescribed for this "obsessive fixation on another person": men were told to get married, or else to have sex frequently with different beautiful women; women were advised to take lots of baths and to distract themselves with food, games, and music. Originally only men were believed to suffer from love sickness, and only later did women learn to suffer from the same malady. "Then it was considered hysteria," Wack says.

Whatever love is, whatever it does to people, there is an increasing awareness that both love and sex remain very important to people as they get older. Many widowed and divorced people who are in good physical and emotional health looking to remate late in middle life — along with large numbers of seniors in their sixties, seventies, and beyond — are seeking more than just companionship and assistance in coping. In resuming a conjugal life, many want a continuation of sexual activity as well. Books such as *Sex After Sixty* by Robert Butler and Myrna Lewis and *The Starr-Wiener Report on Sex and Sexuality in Later Years* are increasingly finding their way to the bookstores.

A four hundred page Consumers Union report titled *Love, Sex, and Aging* surveys the sexual attitudes and practices of more than four thousand Americans aged fifty and over, and it has become a valuable part of the increasing body of research available to guide mature people in the areas of love and sex. The report found that most senior citizens believe "it's okay for older couples who are not married to have sexual relations," though they generally took a dim view of adultery. And despite old teachings inherited from their parents that masturbation is sinful and can lead to physical deformity or insanity, the seniors overwhelmingly agreed that "boys and girls need to be reassured that there is nothing wrong with masturbation" and agreed four to one that masturbation was a "proper" activity for older people. The researchers also found that older couples who continued to engage in sex reported themselves happier than those who didn't. Such findings come as no surprise to dating and relating mature singles.

It is also true that many healthy older couples forgo sex and nevertheless enjoy rewarding companionate love and happy lives together. While it is a useless exercise to judge either practice as being "right" or "wrong," it is a proper question of compatibility facing couples considering remarriage or living together.

REMARRIAGE

Whatever your age, circumstances, background, desires, values, religious beliefs, health, habits — whatever — you can probably find someone with whom to enter a relationship. If you date someone a lot and talk to each other over the phone frequently, and if you become intimate and lean on each other for emotional support, if you eventually begin to see each other almost every day, you will have entered a relationship. This may have come about over a period of weeks or months or else by a stroke of lightning. Where do you go from here? Do you remarry, live together, or just continue to live separately and go steady?

Whether any particular relationship will continue to flourish or will wither away is, of course, impossible to predict; but it will certainly be influenced by the context in which it is maintained. Trust in one another, along with common interests and values, has always been a mainstay for the institution of marriage — and this is true for any kind of relationship.

Unfortunately, half of all marriages — and certainly the majority of other relationships — end before the death of one of the partners. Why? Perhaps our "modern" media-heavy culture makes us all too aware of imagined greener pastures. Judith Martin writes, somewhat tongue-in-cheek, in her excellent book *Miss Manner's Guide to Excruciatingly Correct Behavior*: "There are two distinct classes of people today — not Rich and Poor, but Looking and Not Looking. The overwhelming occupation of the population seems to be looking for a mate, which leaves those who are mated nothing to do but macramé. That is why the latter are so anxious to discuss what is wrong with their relationships: so that they can break up and start all over again."

The new ease with which divorce may be obtained, the increased acceptance of nonmarital cohabitation, and the increasing economic independence of women have all had profound effects on the institution of marriage. Even so, for most of us remarriage probably makes more sense than any other arrangement, provided that certain counter-incentives — often of an economic nature — are not present. For example, should a widow remarry even if it means permanently giving up pension and health benefits she is entitled to by virtue of her deceased husband's employment, or should she opt for a live-in arrangement?

Mature middle-agers may very well find that remarriage introduces a number of considerations they didn't have to deal with when they were first married. Serious couples would do well to read *The Complete Guide to Marriage, Divorce, Custody, and Living Together*, by Steven Mitchell Zack, which lives up to its title. In my opinion, remarriage is the best solution, provided that finances, property matters, and inter-family relations can be worked out ahead of time. Both partners should consult their lawyers.

When we grew up, marriage was the expected outcome of love, and in spite of changing times, it still is. On the other hand, while I personally envy the couples I know who have happily remarried, I have seen many remarried couples divorce, some badly hurt economically as well as emotionally. I nevertheless recommend remarriage if a fair prenuptial arrangement can be agreed to, even though I recognize that all marriages aren't made in heaven and agree with Ann Lander's assessment that "one marriage out of twenty is wonderful, four are good, ten are tolerable, and five are pure hell."

"IN GOD'S EYE" MARRIAGES

Marriages sanctioned by the church occurred earlier than those licensed by the state, and some people are again entering marriages sanctioned *only* by the church, "in God's Eye." Such religious unions require no blood tests, licenses, or state records. Couples may "avoid declaring themselves married for Social Security and tax purposes, and this suits some people just fine," according to Maria Vesperi in an in-depth and enlightening article in the *St. Petersburg Times*. Properly, couples who enter into these unions cannot be considered part of the living-together trend. "Many, if not most, involve widows and widowers who would prefer to marry legally, but can't afford it without the retirement benefits each has earned separately." According to Vesperi, "children can also be a factor, sometimes discouraging their parents from legally remarrying because they are worried about their inheritances." Often the children drop all opposition and even serve as witnesses to the "in God's Eye" ceremonies.

In an interview with the Reverend R.A. Maase of Lawrence, Massachusetts, who is one of the pioneering clergymen performing such marriages, Vesperi learned that the greatest benefit most couples derived was the spiritual relief and good conscience they felt when their union was blessed in a spiritual ceremony. Maase believes that what he is doing has always been sanctioned by the Lord and points out that in Christ's day "there was no such thing as legal marriage; it was a spiritual or religious marriage."

The Reverend Mr. Maase, an Episcopal minister, has experienced a great demand for his services since he was mentioned in a *Dear Abby* column, so great that he has recruited other clergymen to help out. That there is wide support for this practice among other clergymen is indicated by the fact that he received over 900 letters from priests, ministers, and rabbis who sympathized with his work.

Nevertheless, according to Vesperi, most clergy are reluctant to perform such ceremonies. They say they fear possible legal ramifications — although no legal problems were reported by any of the hundreds of couples Maase screened, counseled, and married. Other clergymen refuse to participate because their denominations prohibit or discourage them from doing so. However, Vesperi found that there was agreement among the clergymen that when a couple is married "in God's Eye," they are indeed united spiritually. Even so, a spiritual marriage is not legally recognized, so again it is important that both partners see their respective lawyers to have the financial consequences explained and to have wills and contractual agreements drawn up.

LIVING TOGETHER

English common law used to force marriage on couples living together for a long time, typically at least seven years, by simply recognizing them as husband and wife — with all the legal rights, obligations, and responsibilities pertaining to licensed marriages. In recent years, however, most states have passed laws voiding the legal standing of common-law marriages, though grandfather clauses were sometimes inserted to protect Social Security eligibility and other rights of the then-existing common-law unions.

Though couples who lived together without sanction of the church or state were once few in number, and not at all kindly tolerated by society, this has certainly changed. Much more ignored than rejected or accepted, such unions have mushroomed to the point that the Census Bureau counts POSSLQ's (Persons of the Opposite Sex Sharing Living Quarters) in the millions.

Couples enter into living-together arrangements for different reasons, and for varying periods of time. Such a relationship can last for many years and be every bit as intimate, caring, and committed as a good marriage; or it can be entered into casually, for a brief period, as a matter of convenience. Some couples look upon living together as a means of "testing" to see if getting married would work out. One recent study found that more marriages that were thus "pre-tested" ended in divorce court than those where the couples did not live together first.

Whatever the motives, couples who take this path should see to it that they understand all the legal aspects of such an arrangement. Most of us are familiar with the Hollywood lawsuit some years ago brought against actor Lee Marvin by his former live-in girlfriend. As *Money* magazine pointed out in an article by Patricia O'Toole, "The law is muddy about the individual rights of unmarried couples unless they put their intentions in writing." This, of course, is what mature adults should do if they remate within any of the frameworks described above.

Sometimes one of the partners will balk when the other suggests entering into a pre-living-together (or prenuptial) agreement. The reason often given is that if they don't trust each other enough going in, maybe they ought not to get together at all. Well, maybe not, but an argument can also be made that trust is something you earn as a result of the way you conduct yourself over many years — not something that is simply demanded or bestowed outright.

THE PURSUIT OF HAPPINESS

Whichever path you choose, be it a prelude to remating or to an indefinite single lifestyle, remember that most of the fun is in the everyday living, and that good humor and a sense of humor are indispensable in getting along with others. I used to be so serious about dating and relating. Early on after my divorce, I agonized over every move I was about to make in the dating game, anxious that I might be turned down, certain that tragedy was about to strike. Looking back, what really tended to play out in my post-divorce single life was a comedy that would give any audience a healthy belly laugh if it were scripted for the movies and enacted by a talent like Jack Lemmon.

I still believe that the best destiny for most men and women is to enjoy a long and happy marriage beginning at the dawn of their maturity and extending for many decades until death parts them. There are so many advantages of moving forward together from youth to old age with shared memories of children, vacations, Thanksgiving dinners, and Christmases — as well as the trials and tribulations of life.

Some fortunate couples do enjoy life-long marriages approaching this ideal. They are certainly among the winners, and I tip my hat to them! But other couples also belong in the winners' circle, particularly the happy remarrieds who, having found each other late in life after a death or divorce, regain their footing and finish with flying colors in life's race for happiness. To their numbers must also be added many "in God's Eye" unions, as well as some of the "live-ins" and other couples who live separately but maintain longstanding, caring, and exclusive relationships. Finally, we must certainly include singles who are not in relationships but relate well to others and lead happy and active social lives with the support, love, and friendship of family, friends, dates, and relates in both Real World and Single World.

I have come to understand that unions are not made between perfect angels in heaven, but on earth by imperfect humans. A harder lesson has been the realization that, unlike diamonds, relationships are never forever. However happy, every relationship is destined to come to an end — and life keeps going on, for better or for worse. Where there is a will, however, each ending can be a prelude to a new beginning. Every new relationship can be as rewarding as the last, albeit in a different way.

Remember that in the pursuit of happiness, as with travel to any destination, a lot of the fun is simply in the voyage. So develop new interests, look to your physical, spiritual, and emotional health, widen your friendship circles, date frequently, position yourself appropriately, and be yourself. Let nature take its course as you cruise toward new adventures in dating, relating, and (maybe) remating.

Index